ROWAN

Reaktion's Botanical series is the first of its kind, integrating horticultural and botanical writing with a broader account of the cultural and social impact of trees, plants and flowers.

Published
Apple Marcia Reiss
Ash Edward Parker
Bamboo Susanne Lucas
Berries Victoria Dickenson
Birch Anna Lewington
Cactus Dan Torre
Cannabis Chris Duvall
Carnation Twigs Way
Carnivorous Plants Dan Torre
Cherry Constance L. Kirker and Mary Newman
Chrysanthemum Twigs Way
Geranium Kasia Boddy
Grasses Stephen A. Harris
House Plants Mike Maunder
Lily Marcia Reiss
Mulberry Peter Coles
Oak Peter Young
Orchid Dan Torre
Palm Fred Gray
Pine Laura Mason
Poppy Andrew Lack
Primrose Elizabeth Lawson
Rhododendron Richard Milne
Rose Catherine Horwood
Rowan Oliver Southall
Snowdrop Gail Harland
Sunflowers Stephen A. Harris
Tulip Celia Fisher
Weeds Nina Edwards
Willow Alison Syme
Yew Fred Hageneder

ROWAN

Oliver Southall

REAKTION BOOKS

For Anna

Published by
REAKTION BOOKS LTD
Unit 32, Waterside
44–48 Wharf Road
London N1 7UX, UK
www.reaktionbooks.co.uk

First published 2023
Copyright © Oliver Southall 2023

All rights reserved

No part of this publication may be reproduced, stored in a retrieval
system or transmitted, in any form or by any means, electronic,
mechanical, photocopying, recording or otherwise, without the prior
permission of the publishers

Printed and bound in India by Replika Press Pvt. Ltd

A catalogue record for this book is available from the British Library

ISBN 978 1 78914 712 4

Contents

Rowan on heathland, southern England.

Introduction
Thresholds of Nature and Culture
✤

Most likely, if asked to imagine a rowan, it is the common mountain ash, *Sorbus aucuparia*, that you will call to mind. You might picture, first, a fairly slender overall shape, not too spreading, yet often with many minor trunks – a diminutive tree of medium height. You might picture its smooth, silvery bark and those shimmering pinnate leaves. Almost certainly, you can imagine the frothy corymbs of clotted-cream blossom in spring and that defining burst of late-summer colour as the lightness of flowers gives way to the clustered gravity of scarlet berries. Finally, in autumn, the picture flickers with the sunset palette of its changing leaves.

Intriguingly, the tree we've just conjured, the common mountain ash, though it knows some regional variation and forms numerous hybrids, is the *only* wild species of rowan in most of Eurasia. The mountain ash and other rowan species, most of them confined to mountainous areas of South Central and Southeast Asia, belong to the genus *Sorbus* of the rose family, Rosaceae, and, within that, to the subfamily Maloideae, whose name derives from the Latin *malus*, apple. Unlike the single-stoned drupes of cherries, plums, peaches and almonds or the fleshy achenes formed by wild brambles and strawberries – all also roses – the Maloideae produce fruits with a core. Known as 'pomes', these usually contain two to five seeds. Look again at a rowan berry – it is a tiny scarlet apple.[1]

In the wild, rowans frequently hybridize with other Maloideae. In Europe, mountain ash is part of a hybrid complex that includes the

7

Sorbus aucuparia in its autumn colours.

wild service tree, true service tree and various whitebeams.[2] Based
on this potential to hybridize, numerous trees in the Maloideae have
historically been included in the genus *Sorbus*. The common whitebeam is often known as *Sorbus aria*, while the service trees are *Sorbus
torminalis* and *Sorbus domestica*. In the early 1990s, however, a comprehensive taxonomic study unsettled this classification, proposing that
old associates be bundled into shiny new genera: *Aria* for the whitebeams, *Torminalis* for wild service and *Cormus* for the true service tree.[3]
Despite their hybrids, it turns out, these genera are no more closely
related to one another than to other sections of the subfamily. The
rowans are easily differentiated within the hybrid complex by their
pinnate leaves – and from the true service tree, *Cormus domestica*, by
the size of their fruits.

By 'rowan', then, this book means the pinnate-leaved species of
the revised genus *Sorbus*. For the most part, it will mean the common
mountain ash, a tree left geographically isolated in its genus by the
taxonomic revision just mentioned. Indeed, though *Sorbus*, newly
defined, contains more than ninety species, the majority of these
are confined to mountainous areas of Southeast Asia – from the

Himalayas in Tibet through Sichuan, Yunnan and the mountains of Myanmar and Vietnam. The only other rowan species that come close to the wide spread of *Sorbus aucuparia* are a few ostensibly similar red-fruited varieties: the Japanese rowan, *Sorbus commixtae*, and its North American descendants such as the American rowan, *Sorbus americana*. Other American species, such as *Sorbus sitchensis*, the Sitka rowan, are confined to the western mountains of the continent. There is very little geographic overlap between the Eurasian mountain ash and other rowans.[4]

Rowans come in many shapes and sizes. Some rowans are tall, reaching 30 m (100 ft) in height; others, such as the diminutive *Sorbus poteriifolia*, are dwarf shrubs, and spread by rhizomes. Flowers and berries offer further variety. *Sorbus filipes* carry corymbs of dark crimson blooms, while in other species the blossoms range through shades of pink to pure white. Berries, likewise, can be snowy pale in species such as *Sorbus fruticosa* and *Sorbus koehneana*, but range through many pink and pink-spotted varieties to the more familiar yellows,

Harvest of pomes
from *Sorbus aucuparia*.

9

oranges and reds of *Sorbus aucuparia*. The size, shape and number of the pinnate leaflets are additionally variable, as is their autumn colouration. *Sorbus setschwaniensis* is notable for many pairs of tiny leaflets, while *Sorbus harrowiana* has just two or three, each large and club-shaped. *Sorbus rehderiana* carries glossy, wine-dark leaves in autumn, while cultivars such as 'Joseph Rock' and 'sp. Ghose' are prized by gardeners for their vibrant displays of whisky and vermilion flame.

Thanks to their diversity of form, colour and texture, and the year-round interest they provide, rowans are popular trees with gardeners and urban planners. Often planted as 'amenity' trees, bringing life to grey winter streets, the rarer rowans are also prized specimens in northern European botanical gardens, harking back to an age of colonial exploration and plunder. But the promise of new and

Young leaves on a seedling of *Sorbus aucuparia*.

Sitka mountain ash (*Sorbus sitchensis*) near Mount Rainier, Washington.

attractive varieties is not the only lure of plant-collecting expeditions, for, as well as its significance for horticulture, the peculiar distribution of the rowans offers a compelling puzzle for botanical science. Why such a starkly absolute divide in the geographic distribution of the genus, a vast stretch of Eurasia dominated by just one species and then this isolated mountain hinterland of concentrated genetic variety?

To answer this question requires a reconstruction of the evolution of *Sorbus*. Rowans don't offer much fossil evidence beyond the end of the last ice age – about 15,000 years ago – but a few avenues of inquiry are available: careful study of the genus's current distribution; comparison of the evolutionary journey of ecologically associated species, such as birch; a bit of educated guesswork.[5] The likely story begins in the Eocene – 54 to 36 million years ago – when broad-leaved deciduous trees, related to birch and alder, began to evolve in the widespread forests of dawn redwood, ginkgo, larch and swamp cypress. Despite the absence of fossils, it's probable that the first

top: The popular garden cultivar 'Joseph Rock'.

middle: Distinctive white-fruited rowans such as *Sorbus koehneana* (pictured) are found only in mountainous areas of southern Asia.

bottom: Leaves and berries of *Sorbus fruticosa*.

Urban rowan, King's
Cross, London.

Urban rowan, King's
Cross, London.

primitive rowans emerged at this time, and the nature and placement
of current species offer some intriguing hints. In parts of China and
Vietnam, relict pockets of forest related to the Eocene woods cling
on, offering opportunities for botanists to make deep time journeys
of evolutionary discovery. In 1997, an expedition to Fan Si Pan, a
mountain in North Vietnam, revealed a new endemic species of rowan,
duly named as *Sorbus fansipanensis*. These isolated trees were growing
with a birch, *Betula insignis*, which is similar to fossils of Eocene birches
and was found to be almost evergreen – a likely characteristic of the
earliest deciduous species. Another species, *Sorbus wilsoniana*, has also
been found with *Betula insignis* on Mount Fanjing in Guizhou, China,
another recognized location for ancestral forest. Might these species
be the closest living relatives of the first recognizable rowans? It is a
compelling possibility.

If we accept that *Sorbus* first emerged in the Eocene mountains of what is now Southwest Asia, then rowans were probably confined to mountain areas for much of their subsequent evolutionary history. Today, most rowans are well adapted to life at altitude, but only weakly competitive with lower-growing forest-forming species such as those that dominated the Eocene globe. Deep in the Eocene, India started to collide with Asia, raising the Himalayas. But Eocene Asia also had its pre-existing ranges which, being orientated on a north–south axis, would have offered the first rowans some opportunity to spread through different climactic regions defined by latitude, gradually diversifying the genus. It is likely that this was the slow pattern throughout the Oligocene and Miocene (up to 6 million years ago). The development of the Japanese rowan (*Sorbus commixta*) and its journey into North America is typically dated to this period. Only later, as the Himalayas pushed ever upwards, growing separate from more northerly ranges as well as more geographically distinct in their own prominences, would diverse species come to be isolated in their islands of altitude.

We have to wait until the Pleistocene (2 million to 15,000 years before the present), when Earth's climate cooled and periodic ice ages became a major ecological factor, for *Sorbus aucuparia*'s big moment. When it came, the Pleistocene ice cleared vast areas of temperate forest, especially in northern Europe, and offered opportunities for cold-adapted species, particularly those that could disperse rapidly, to colonize new areas. Rowan, whose seed is most commonly spread by birds, certainly fits the bill. Analysis of lake-sediment pollen deposits in the Outer Hebrides and southern Sweden have shown the presence of mountain ash in the early Holocene as forests returned. On the Isle of Lewis, the tree was present in open woodlands of birch and hazel, which began to form around 9,500 years ago. These woods gradually succumbed to blanket peat as the climate became wet and cooled.[6] In Sweden, rowan was part of mixed deciduous upland forest with oak, elm, lime and beech; its berries likely helped feed the first Mesolithic settlers in the area.[7]

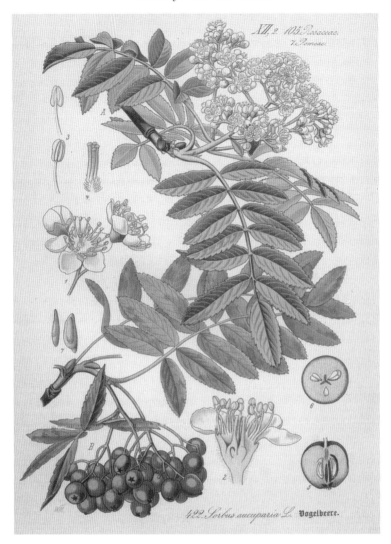

Sorbus aucuparia, illustration from Otto Wilhelm Thomé, *Flora von Deutschland, Österreich und der Schweiz*, vol. III (1888).

While we can be fairly sure that rowan played an important role in forest succession after the ice ages, we are still left with the question of why only one species, *Sorbus aucuparia*, seems to have spread widely. A few factors come into play here. First, there is the question of the trees' ability to descend from their mountain haunts. In the mountains of Asia, where *Sorbus* is now most diverse, it may be that the climate was always sufficiently warm to ensure that temperate forest formed a barrier to the dispersal of rowans: trees would tend to be isolated in separate ranges, granting only those species that had spread to more northerly mountains an opportunity to colonize lower-lying areas. This is probably what distinguished the common rowan and the few species now in East Asia and North America.

The spread of *Sorbus aucuparia* seems to have been comparatively recent. It is absent from North America, so the slow explosion of its population must have happened after the closure of the most recent suitable land bridge with Asia, around 2 to 3 million years ago. Significantly, the tree is self-compatible – able to pollinate itself and form viable fruit. Self-compatibility of this sort is thought to result from a genetic bottleneck in the evolutionary history of a species, implying a period of geographic confinement followed by rapid spread. A picture develops in which *Sorbus aucuparia* emerged from a long-isolated species clinging on in some mountain fastness of northern Eurasia – until,

Sorbus aucuparia, Glen Loyne, Scotland.

at some point, receding ice gave it a chance to spread and so saved it from likely extinction. If this is true, then rowan is an unlikely survivor, rescued in the nick of epochal time. Though we often think of evolutionary history as purely defined by competitive pressures – as a long, iterative and inexorable march to perfect adaptation – the rowan reminds us that it is also a story of contingency, fragility and chance.

Much of the reconstruction of rowan's deep history is based on an understanding of the tree's current ecology. The Eurasian rowan is a lover of mountains and rocky places, a pioneer into opened ground. In Britain, it is far more common and prominent in the wetter mountainous regions of the north and west than it is in the warmer lowland counties of the southeast. Being well adapted to a short summer growing season, and tolerating severe desiccation of its buds during freezing winters, rowan can be found higher up mountains than any other British tree.[8] A specialist of craggy situations with very little soil, rowan adds drama to many a vertiginous scene. Where it roots itself on rocks and cliffs, the tree often grows initially downwards before curving towards the light, it can form impressive webs of muscular, anchoring roots, clasping rock and guying into crevices. Across Europe, the picture is the same, with lonely rowans growing above the forest limit in most countries – up to 2,000 m (6,560 ft) in France and 1,500 m (4,900 ft) further north in Norway. In a study of tree-limit changes in the Swedish Scandes mountains, 52 per cent of identified rowan specimens were growing in soil-less boulder fields; 31 per cent were spotted on slopes practically inaccessible to humans and to larger herbivores such as moose, whose predilection for its tender young leaves severely limits the tree's abundance.[9]

Rowans stand out at high altitudes and as lone trees of cliffs, crags and screes. Lower down, where it merges into woodland, the rowan rarely forms pure stands, appearing more often as a scattered presence in mountain woods and in areas of boreal and hemi-boreal forest. In

Rowan clinging to a hillside boulder, Raasay, Scotland.

the latter, rowan is most common where the dominance of pine and spruce is disrupted by broken ground, especially near rivers and lakes, and in the early stages of forest succession.[10] In such places, rowan is an associate of birch, alder and willow – all species that grow fast and tolerate difficult soil conditions. In Britain, the rowan is an important tree species in upland ash woods of the northwest, as well as in mixed oak and birch woodland on sandy soils.[11] In such situations, it is especially frequent where land-use patterns have changed and heath or wood-pasture has begun to revert to woody scrub due to the absence of grazing animals. Rowan can be found in the distinctive lowland beech forests of southern Scandinavia and northern and central Europe, as well as in high beech woods of mountain areas in central and southern Europe.[12] In woodland, seedlings are able to germinate and survive in a slow-growing suppressed state – a kind of protracted adolescence. In the right conditions, such trees can be found in large numbers, waiting for a gap to open in the canopy.[13]

Both its opportunist ability to colonize new areas and its frequent occurrence in apparently inaccessible locations are the result of rowan's ecological association with birds – the principal dispersers of its seed. A study of ruminant impact on plant communities in Welsh hill-pastures found that when grazing was curtailed, rowan seedlings were notably present along fence lines: the posts were acting as perches for birds, which eat the berries and deposit the seed.[14] In wooded situations, rowan may benefit from the tendency of birds to sit on dead trees. A concentration of germinating seedlings in such spots enables rowan to quickly exploit newly available light.[15] (Rowans are also remarkably adept at growing epiphytically on rotting wood, slowly reaching their roots into the soil below; such a strategy may be an adaptation to escape browsing pressures.) Many bird species are drawn to the rowan's bright pomes, from thrushes, finches and waxwings to smaller birds such as robins, tits and even some warblers. The fruit is small enough to be swallowed whole.[16] Yearly crops of rowan berries have a recognized impact on bird migrations. When rowans in Scandinavia, Finland and Russia are heavily laden with fruit, breeding fieldfare will delay their movement into warmer parts of Europe; rowan berries are an important food for migrating redwing and ring ouzel.[17]

Fluctuations in the rowan berry crop in northern latitudes is crucial, too, in explaining the irregular, irruptive migrations of waxwings into Britain and Ireland. While in most years these boldly marked and audaciously coiffed passerines visit Britain only in small

overleaf: A flock of waxwing feeds on frozen rowan berries.

numbers – and are largely confined to the north and east of the archipelago – some winters they arrive in their thousands, flocks of them, moving gradually south and west to feast on fruit and berries in city streets, gardens and woods. The behaviour is complex, but ornithological research has shown it to be intimately related to the size and distribution of the rowan fruit in the birds' breeding areas.[18] In the year following an especially heavy fruiting, an enlarged wax-wing population may coincide with exhaustion of the trees; struggling for food, the surplus birds are forced out from their usual range, sometimes heading west to the Atlantic edges of the continent. Conversely, in years in which the winter crop is unusually large, the waxwing may be outcompeted by lingering fieldfare, another stimulus to greater migratory range.

We often think of animal migration as giving us access to stable and ancient patterns of life – to a realm of planetary integration and seasonal recurrence that transcends the chaos, pace and unpredictability of human society. Waxwing movements offer a different perspective – perhaps closer to that of migrant humans in our global world – of opportunism and risk, of the defining force of need, and the fragility of any individual life: a waxwing ringed in Aberdeen during the winter

Avenue of urban rowans, Enfield, north London.

22

invasion of 2004–5 perished the following winter nearly 4,000 km (2,485 mi.) away – it was killed by a domestic cat in a hamlet on the western Siberian plain.[19]

To the flock of chattering waxwings feasting on berries, the fruited rowans on a suburban road are not diminished by their decorative, civic placement; they are a crucial lifeline and a link in a wild chain that sweeps across continents. Next time you pass a laden winter rowan in the street, let it unlimit your perspective for a moment, entering the bird's-eye view – millions of bright beacons stretching thousands of kilometres, a red thread stitched through hidden and unbordered worlds.

The rowan's capacity to act as a threshold to other realms has been historically central to cultural significations of the tree – the fertile crossings of its natural existence with the ever-changing beliefs, values and perceptions of human societies. So far, we have looked at rowan in a broadly scientific manner, considering its taxonomic placement, evolutionary phytogeography and ecological relationships. While dry and technical at times, such classificatory approaches also connect us to deeper questions of how we look at and organize our world – how we decide which things can be meaningfully related to one another and in what ways, which properties we prioritize as defining the identity of a natural object and how we perceive space and make sense of time.

For contemporary scientists, the classification of living nature is largely a matter of genes. The most meaningful taxonomic information exists at the microscopic level of the chromosome and the challenge is to see past superficial forms of likeness between organisms. Reflecting this systematic differentiation of species, the standard binomial name, *Sorbus aucuparia*, encodes a precise phylogenetic placement, laying claim to a timeless state of knowledge.

In contrast to the taxonomic Latin, vernacular monikers are a living archive of diverse and ever-shifting ways of seeing – a cultural ecology affording an indicative glimpse into the dynamic nature of human perception. Many of the vernacular names given to rowan are records of simple noticing. 'Mountain ash', for example, alerts us to both a specialist habitat of the tree and the likeness of its pinnate foliage to that of ash (*Fraxinus excelsior*). In Romance languages, most names for the tree are derived from Latin *sorbus*, from which we also get 'service tree'. These names, such as the Italian *sorbo* and Spanish *serbal*, encode the historic recognition of rowan's likeness to the service tree, *Cormus domestica*. The German *Vogelbeer*, or 'bird-berry', is also a form of ecological attention, making note of the tree's allure for winter birds. The French *sorbier des oiseleurs*, 'bird-catcher's service', supplements this knowledge with a reference to its practical exploitation: it reminds us of the tree's utility as a lure for trappers of edible songbirds. The Russian *ryabina* is enigmatic, but may derive from Slavic words for the hazel grouse (*Bonasa bonasia*), a ground-nesting bird of the taiga and of mixed deciduous forest for which rowan berries are an important autumn food; a possible semantic derivation would be something along the lines of 'grouse-berry'.[20]

In many northern European languages, vernacular names for rowan are related to the redness of the tree's berries. The German word *Eberesche* evolved from an Indo-European root meaning red, while *rowan*, a word of Scandinavian origin – and thus a reminder of Viking settlement in Scotland and northern England – derives from an Old Norse colour-word *rauðr*.[21] Now the most widespread English name, *rowan* was largely a feature of northern dialects until the nineteenth century, knowing many variant pronunciations and spellings: *rantry*, *rauntry*, *rown-tree*, *roan-tree*, *round-tree*.[22] It is also the source of a common English surname – Rowntree.

In the etymological depths of such words, we access an ancestral field of vision in which the rowan was defined, most of all, as a member of the genus *Natural things that are red*. For ancient peoples of northern Europe, this primal association of rowan with redness surely held more than aesthetic significance: the deep anthropological importance of this colour helps explain a widespread European belief in the rowan's magical potency – its protective power, its status as a threshold between worlds. For most archaic peoples, red was more than a colour. Red, in fact, has a good claim to be called the first colour in human culture. Linguists have discovered a near universal progression of colour terms in the development of languages: in almost all lexica it is the word for red that first differentiates the quality of hue from that of brightness – from light and dark, black and white.[23] As a primordial term in the human experience of tint, it is unsurprising that red has a religious significance stretching back millennia. One of the oldest ceremonial burials discovered in Europe, the so-called Red Lady – actually a Palaeolithic man whose remains date to circa 32,000 BCE – was placed in a cave wearing a red-dyed ceremonial garment.[24] Stone-age burial practices seem commonly to have involved the sprinkling of red ochre, while paintings on cave walls and ritual figurines also make use of the colour, produced through the heating of yellow ochre or extracted from haematite.[25] Red may have been considered a protective colour, or it may have been associated with passage from one world to the next, to a realm of ancestors and spirits. Either way, red's ancient ritual significance must have been intimately linked to its universal associations with fire and blood – elemental forces of life, but also of death and destruction.[26] Blood has symbolic potency as a shorthand for fertility, kinship and sacrifice. Associated with menstruation and birth, it symbolizes the passage from spirit into flesh; in sacrificial rites, the direction of travel is reversed, with blood serving as a communicative conduit with supernatural realms. Fire, too, has long been associated with processes of transformation and spiritual knowledge: bringing life and warmth, it can also destroy and overwhelm.

In its symbolic associations, as we shall see, red rowan participates in the full range of connotations carried by its signal colour: it is emblematic of natural beauty; it marks and opens borders between worlds; it offers spiritual nourishment and replenishment of life and,

overleaf: The redness of rowan is a significant factor in the etymology of its vernacular names and the tree's symbolism in myth and folklore.

while it guards against danger and magical threat, it can also be a potent and destructive force. Celtic words for rowan reveal a primary association with fire. Cognate words around the Scottish Gaelic *caorunn* offer striking evidence both of rowan's prominence in the Highland imagination and of a language tightly woven to a particular ecology. The Gaelic noun *caor* can be used as a generic term for any globular red mass, connecting the berries of rowan with a range of hot or luminescent substances. Likewise, the adjective *caorach*, 'abounding in berries', has secondary metaphorical meanings of flaming heat, sparkle or scintillation, even hot-temperedness.[27]

Throughout the Celtic cultural domain, rowan was long believed to have magical potency. In the Scottish Highlands, at the opening of summer, rowan was a component of the Beltane fires used to bless and protect the herds before their annual departure for higher pastures: Celtic pastoralists have historically thought the wood especially useful in protecting cattle and their milk from bewitchment and fairy theft.[28] The prominence of rowan in Celtic areas of the British Isles has also allowed the tree to serve as a focus for artistic negotiations of national identity in these regions – ecological and cultural geographies strategically intertwined in an argument for regional self-definition. Indeed, as a tree associated with remoteness, with mountainous and less fertile land, rowan has its place in the negotiation of marginal identities across its European range. In addition to its emblematic place in the articulation of Celtic nationalisms, rowan featured prominently in Finnish arguments for independence in the nineteenth and early twentieth centuries. In Finnish, which is part of the Uralic language group, the tree is known as *pihlaja*.

Other vernacular names for rowan also highlight the tree's association with spiritual power. 'Quickbeam' and 'quicken tree' are words derived from Old English *cwic-beam*.[29] Similar names, such as *Quickenbaum* and *Quitschenbaum*, survive in northern German dialects.[30] The origins of these cognates are uncertain but seem to include the sense of 'quick' as alive or full of vitality – as in the biblical phrase 'the quick and the dead'. Reference to the use of *cwic-beam*, assumed by many scholars to be rowan, is found in West Saxon charms for reviving infertile land, confirming the tree's connection with a magical life-force.[31]

From quickbeam, we also have *wicken* or *wiggen tree*, more common in northern Britain (and behind the tree's prominence in the coat of arms of the city of Wigan). Such names seem to conflate the root word *quicken* with terms derived from the Old English *wic*, indicating pliancy (as with the willow shoots used in *wicker*). Scattered evidence that rowan was once considered a useful wood for bows may explain the linguistic development. It is certainly an indicator of the pliancy of language, the human ability to weave meanings through connections of sound and sense. Similar folk-etymological transformations of the Anglo-Saxon root have also produced names such as *witchwood*, *witchen* and *witch-wicken*: they preserve a memory of rowan's use in protective magic and charms against witchcraft, but they also acknowledge that magic power may be appropriated for darker purposes. Finally, we have variants of *whitty-* or *whitten-tree*, names that advertise the whiteness of the tree's blossom. These names may also apply to the whitebeam and to white-flowered viburnums such as wayfaring tree and guelder rose. Again, varied vernacular usage posits its own genus, a grouping based on lived experience of floral relationships rather than strict genetic accuracy.

'Language', wrote the American philosopher and poet Ralph Waldo Emerson, 'is fossil poetry.'[32] Words, as Emerson saw them, are repositories of imaginative life: they act as vessels for the associative power of mind, a force drawn from the manifold interactions of sensation with its world, the boundless desire to communicate experience and emotion. The many and varied words for rowan are a tiny part of the endlessly imbricated process of linguistic emergence. Yet to delve into the origins of just these few terms is to see that language lives because words participate in culture: they are sedimented with history, encoding priorities of noticing informed by past practices and beliefs.

In the 1950s, the French literary critic Roland Barthes gave the provocative name 'mythologies' to the social significations at play in everyday symbols and images. Refusing the anthropological separation of 'modern' from 'primitive' societies – the one governed by rational law, the other by myth – Barthes argued that even the most trivial aspects of our everyday lives could be animated by rich and largely unconscious layers of 'mythological' association.[33] This is a book about the 'mythology' of rowan in that expanded sense. It explores how the things among which we live – landscapes, places, plants, animals and trees – give shape to our understanding of longing

Gilded rowan armchair, c. 1828, designed by Karl Friedrich Schinkel.

and belonging, to our visions of history, to our sense of uncertainty or fear, joy and hope.

Just as we need stories that offer comfort and consolation, finding shared meaning in plants, animals and places is fundamental to our capacity for solidarity and co-belonging. In his great writings on the Aran Islands off Ireland's west coast, the cartographer and writer Tim Robinson revealed in extraordinary detail how even the smallest and most isolated stretch of habitable land could be an endlessly layered repository of human stories, an archive of anthropological under-standing. Having moved to Aran in the 1970s, Robinson gradually conceived of a work in which these islands would serve as an 'exem-plary terrain' for thinking the human relationship with nature in its dizzyingly intricate complexity: they were small enough to gradually reveal all the rich stratigraphy of myth, yet big enough and, crucially, beautiful enough to have exercised a powerful imaginative hold on all who had inhabited and visited them.[34]

In an imaginary ethnobotanical atlas, I'd like to suggest, the rowan might occupy an analogous place to Robinson's islands. Rather than forming a vast continent of story and lore, surviving cultural engagements with rowan are limited enough in extent and number to be considered more of an archipelago in the swirling currents of narrated history. The rowan is not a tree whose first importance to humans has been practical in a directly mechanical sense. Its special fascination and power – ritual and magical, aesthetic and emblematic – derive mainly from its beauty, its unusual taxonomic characteristics and its predilection for precarious and remote locations.

This is not to say that no practical use has been made of the rowan. In his *Sylva* (1664), the English writer and forester John Evelyn noted the hardness and close-grained density of rowan heartwood. Though it is too small to be a significant timber tree, this quality has historically made rowan of some value for carving and turning and in the making of tool handles, wheels and agricultural implements such as yokes and harnesses.[35] 'Fletchers', Evelyn adds, 'commend it for bows next to yew'; a contemporary survival guide for boys corroborates his view.[36] In Scandinavia, the wood has commonly been used for sled parts, a fact alluded to in Finland's national epic, the *Kalevala*.[37] Burning hot and slow, rowan makes excellent firewood.

Historically, the berries, leaves and bark of rowan have also been used in dyeing, providing pigments ranging from yellow to dark red and black. Within the dyeing process, rowan-derived products make effective mordants or fixatives.[38] In northern Scandinavia, shavings of rowan bark were once an important source of food for grazing animals in lean winter months. In Russia, rowan berries have long been considered of pharmacological value, with an entire volume of the compendious *State Pharmacopoeia* dedicated to their uses as a vitamin source, a diuretic and an anti-inflammatory and vasoprotective medicine.[39] Reminiscing on a country childhood, a Soviet writer of the 1960s remembered sprigs of autumn rowan being hung in the eaves so the berries would freeze throughout the winter. The frost-treated berries could then be taken, pill-like, 'as a cure for carbon dioxide poisoning from the fumes of a carelessly heated stove, and for headaches'.[40] Today, dried rowan berries are available in some Russian pharmacies as a multivitamin.[41] In Austria, rowan fruit is used in teas, syrups and jellies to treat the symptoms of cold and flu, as it is rich in vitamin C.[42] 'The juice of the berries', Evelyn noted, 'makes an excellent drink against the spleen and scurvy.'[43]

Though closely connected to such medicinal preparations, the culinary use of rowan berries is not limited to the pharmacological. 'Ale and beer brew'd with these berries', Evelyn adds, 'is an incomparable drink, familiar in Wales.'[44] A century later, John Lightfoot referred to the use of rowan berries to provide 'acid for punch' in Jura. In the

A 'skave' tool used in northern Norway for scraping the bark off rowans, crucial winter fodder for grazing animals.

German stamp, *c.* 1910, showing the liqueur factory Gottlieb Vetter and its rowan berry concoction.

Highlands, Lightfoot claimed, the locals distilled 'a very good spirit from them'.[45] In the nineteenth century, a number of writers, including the novelist Elizabeth Gaskell, noted a homemade Welsh brew, *diod griafol*, made by steeping crushed rowan berries in water.[46] Perhaps this was the same 'familiar' concoction referred to by Evelyn.

In the UK at least, though rowan berries are still used in jellies for the accompaniment of game and for adding bitter accents to jams, such historic enthusiasm for a rowan-berry tipple seems not to have been sustained. My own experiments have produced a passable, if slightly penitential, liquor – and that only on the addition of alarming quantities of sugar. By 'incomparable', of course, Evelyn may not have meant incomparably tasty: the fruit is remarkably astringent and contains compounds that may be poisonous unless cooked. Nowadays, in fact, any rowan-derived chemicals in your drink are likely to be preservatives. In 1859, a German chemist, A. W. von Hofmann, isolated sorbic acid by distillation from the oil of unripe rowan berries. In the next century, the potential of the chemical as an antimicrobial agent was discovered, and it began to be synthesized industrially. In the United States, it was patented for use as a preservative in 1945. Flavourless, safely metabolized and highly effective at inhibiting mould, it is now one of the most widely used chemicals in food

Aesthetic appreciation of rowan: Maurice Pillard Verneuil, *Sorbier*, colour lithograph from Eugène Grasset, ed., *La Plante et ses applications ornementales*, vol. II (1901).

transportation and storage, making global food markets possible.[47] It is a significant twist in rowan's long history as a tree of protection.

Despite their waning popularity in Britain, rowan-flavoured drinks remain common across northern and Alpine Europe. The berries are an important ingredient in Danish Gammel Dansk bitters, in Polish Jarzębiak (an infused vodka), in Austrian Vogelbeerschnaps and in the Finnish fortified wine Sorbus, to name just a few.[48] Aside from its economic importance as a gardener's favourite, as an 'amenity tree' in cities and as the natural inventor of one of our most commonly used preservatives, rowan's greatest contribution to that main deity of contemporary myth – GDP – may well be in such bibulous form.

Mostly though, the rowan is a tree whose mythological significance is related to more intangible qualities. For this reason, much of this book is focused on literature and art, an arena of cultural work

Many artists have responded to the rowan's striking colour and form: Paul Gauguin, *Bouquet de sorbier*, 1884, oil on canvas.

in which the tree has been of considerable importance. Rather than providing a series of thematic samplers of tree lore, *Rowan* sets out to tell a continuous story of social change as focused by literary, artistic and folkloric appearances of the common mountain ash. It is therefore organized in an essentially chronological fashion. In the next chapter, we examine the appearance of rowan in a variety of mythical and pseudo-historical narratives from the Irish and Scandinavian traditions. Although they likely had some connection to ancient oral lore, many of these stories survive in written form only as they were copied down – and likely subtly altered – by early medieval monks, monastic scholars and Christian court poets. In reading them, we ask what they might reveal about archaic religions and their relationship to landscape ecology, but we also focus on how the symbolism of rowan allowed Christian writers to negotiate the pagan past within a new religious culture.

Turning to practical lore and popular belief, Chapter Two examines rowan's history as a tree of safety and reassurance in inhospitable and rugged places, exploring the relationship of rowan's perceived magic power to the charged divisions of social space. In Chapters Three and Four, we learn how, from the eighteenth century, rowan found its place in a range of important literary and artistic movements: in proto-Romantic articulations of cultural nationalism, as well as in works of ecological realism deriving force from the Romantic veneration of nature. Chapter Five carries us into the twentieth century, exploring the significance of rowan in Russia's post-Revolutionary literature of exile and displacement. In Chapter Six, we look at writing and art that deal with land-use change and rural-to-urban migration, as well as poetry and religious anthropology that draw on occult associations of the tree to forge personal, counter-cultural mythologies. Finally, in the conclusion, we consider the tree's future as a source and symbol of ecological regeneration.

The rowan has participated in many of the great social and cultural upheavals of the modern era: industrialization and agricultural intensification; secularization and disenchantment; enclosure and clearance; revolution and war. Through all these shifts and ruptures, the tree's meanings proliferate and branch: as a symbol of political nostalgia and regional resistance to internal colonization, as a mark of detailed attention to local ecologies, as a talisman for the displaced and dispossessed, and as an embodiment of powerful longings for the re-enchantment and restoration of nature. It is my hope that, taken together, the stories I tell with rowan will gradually reveal the rich and intriguing part that something so apparently simple as a tree can play in our collective earthbound life.

Francis Hayman, *The Druids; or, The Conversion of the Britons to Christianity*, 1752, engraving. Classical sources identified the Druids as the custodians of Celtic religion in Britain. In Ireland, the rowan came to be known as *fid na ndruad* — the Druid's tree.

one

Old Gods, New Myths

꩜

A jealous lover, the daughter of a famous Druid, curses her rival with a rowan wand. A god, crossing a river into giant-land, is swept up in a flood, only to be rescued by a rowan growing from the bank. A warrior and his men are lured into a threatening otherworld, its entrance marked by a ring of rowans. A Druid of terrifying power invokes a mysterious deity over a rowan-wood fire.

What can such episodes, all from myth-like narratives written down in medieval Ireland and Scandinavia, tell us about the place of rowan in the deep history of the northern European imagination? Until relatively recently, scholars and philologists saw such stories as a window into archaic religion, puzzles to be deciphered using the tools of comparative mythology and speculative archaeology. Though late to be recorded, they argued, these strange tales originated in oral lore stretching back into pre-history. Interpreted in this manner, they would license us to see the rowan as a tree of great spiritual significance to ancient Celtic and Scandinavian peoples, a conduit between the material and spiritual realms.

Nowadays, we are usually advised to be more circumspect. Even the idea of a Norse or Celtic 'mythology' must be handled with caution.[1] Indeed, much of what we are accustomed to think of as myth, though likely containing remnants of sophisticated oral culture, was only written down after conversion to Christianity. In Ireland, where monasteries thrived as places of literacy and learning, the church hierarchy was legally established by the end of the sixth century; across the Viking world, Christianization began in the late tenth century. To encounter rowan in this literature, then, is to find it at one of many thresholds – a border, always being re-negotiated, between Christian present and pagan past.

The early Christians adopted a range of strategies for displacing and subsuming native paganisms. Though frequently militant, painting local deities as devils and desecrating shrines, they also exploited aspects of theology that allowed a more assimilationist approach. Through its cults of saints and martyrs, the theology of angels and

Page from *The Book of the Dun Cow* (*Lebor na hUidre*), begun *c.* 1106, the oldest surviving monastic compilation of early Irish literature.

devils, the Church was able to absorb many of the impulses behind
pagan beliefs: veneration of sacred places, the wish to plead for fortune from a local god and a belief in spirit-peoples hidden in the
landscape.[2] This chapter examines the mythology of rowan in a tran-
sitional period, as poets and scribes adapted native lore to Christian
frameworks, fitting it to new ideological needs. It was a delicate,
dangerous negotiation, full of fascination and repulsion, of the desire
to preserve and obscure the pagan past. As we shall see, it is just such
uncertainties that animate the literary life of rowan in a corpus of
sagas and tales that continue to inspire and intrigue.

Along with Cú Chulainn, hero of the Ulster Cycle, the best-known
figure in early Irish literature is the seer-poet, occasional buffoon and
charismatic leader of a nomad war-band Fionn Mac Cumhaill (Finn
McCool). Tales of Finn have been part of Gaelic storytelling for many
centuries, with folklorists collecting new versions well into the 1800s.
Unusually for such a rich tradition, however, Fenian lore seems not
to have developed into written form before the twelfth century; it is
a belatedness that has puzzled scholars and may reveal something
important about Christian perceptions of the tales.

Fían bands such as Finn's, nomadic groups of landless mercenaries
who existed in a state of near lawlessness, were a feature of Irish life
until the ninth century and were likely a bastion of pagan lore; indeed,
it is possible that the talismanic figure of Finn derives from a pagan
divinity, 'Vindos', patron of bandit soldiers.[3] Might the Fenian stories
have been a little too virulently pagan for early Christian writers to
handle? If so, Finn tales may contain the best evidence for the
possible significance of rowan to ancient Irish pagans.

Certainly, there is much in these stories to tantalize readers
intrigued by archaic religion. The Finn of myth appears as a kind of

overleaf: Rowans and rainbow in Strathcarron, Scotland. In early Irish
stories, rowans often mark a threshold to magical and mysterious otherworlds.

shaman.[4] He has a special connection with the spirit realm, possessing a tooth and thumb of knowledge, which gift him the power of prophecy. In the Finn Cycle, the rowan is especially associated with a group of adventures known as *bruidhean* (hostel or banquet hall) tales: stories in which Finn and his men are lured into a parallel dimension through the fairy-tale device of some attractive residence in a remote place. Usually, the narrative action of these tales involves a brutal inversion of the rites of hospitality. In one chilling example, told in an untitled twelfth-century manuscript poem known as 'Finn and the Phantoms', Finn is trapped in such a hostel by a giant and subjected to a litany of ghoulish offences. The culmination is the perfunctory slaughter of Finn's horses, their meat served up on magical spits of rowan wood.[5]

Some kind of otherworld – a parallel dimension inhabited by ambiguous spiritual beings – is a prominent feature of Irish tales.[6] Rowans often mark the threshold of this spectral realm, being magically exploited by its inhabitants, who are variously identified as fairies, demons, fallen but repentant angels or a race of semi-divine 'god-peoples' (the mysterious *Tuatha dé*). The spirit realm of the Finn tales, however, possesses a distinctly antagonistic atmosphere. Unlike other, more obviously Christian stories, in which a voyage to the otherworld is a source of illumination or spiritual enlightenment, here it is a place of horror and painful self-knowledge. These singular qualities have led some scholars to speculate that Finn's otherworld might retain traces of archaic, quasi-shamanic beliefs.[7] The *bruidhean*, alluring yet deadly, is central to such arguments, its ambiguous status possibly reflecting the complex relationship between the shaman and his spirit helpers, with whom he negotiates at significant personal risk.[8]

Both the slippery nature of the *bruidhean* and the sacrificial aspect of shamanic quest are alluded to in *Bruidhean Chaorthainn* (literally, 'The Hostel of the Rowans'), a story especially redolent of rowan's otherworldly associations. In this story, Finn and his men are lured into an otherworld hall under the pretext of reconciliation with an enemy, Midac. The hall's enchanted status is signalled by the trees encircling it: 'As Finn and his party came nigh to the palace, they were amazed at its size and splendour . . . It stood on a level green, which was surrounded by a light plantation of quicken trees, all covered with clusters of scarlet berries.'[9] Inside the hall is a vision of lavish hospitality: a 'great fire' blazing in the hearth, couches laid with 'rich coverlets . . . soft, glossy furs', vast banqueting tables.[10] But enchantment soon turns sinister. The fire, initially 'clear and smokeless', fills the hall with a suffocating 'cloud of black, sooty smoke'; the very building is revealed to be 'nothing but rough planks, clumsily fastened . . . with tough quicken tree withes'; the carpets and couches vanish and Finn is magically fastened to 'the bare damp earth . . . cold as the snow'.[11] As Finn and company face the possibility of death, the narrative focus shifts, suddenly, to the mundane external world. A series of battles occurs outside the hostel, as Finn's men fight to save him from annihilation by spiritual fire. Eventually, the dashing Diarmuid comes to the rescue, breaking into the *bruidhean* and sprinkling his enemies' blood to sever the enchantment.

One cross-cultural image in stories concerning shamanic experience is the transformation of the seer into the food of spirit beings, the process of being eaten serving as a metaphor for the pain of gaining otherworldly knowledge.[12] The *Bruidhean Chaoirthainn* retains a tantalizing trace of this idea, as Finn, thinking he is attending a banquet, finds himself literally being roasted alive – becoming the banquet. If we're prepared to accept an archaic link between rowan and a shamanic realm of spirits, we might imagine ancient Celtic seers using rowan berries in their rites or seeking out remote trees as a place for ritual action. It has been suggested that the *bruidhean* is an echo of the sacred grove as sacrificial compound, a place where the gods would feast on burnt offerings.[13] The rowan's tendency to grow alone in isolated spots – especially at high altitude, a traditionally numinous zone – surely made it liable to such otherworldly associations; the belief that 'lone bushes' were sacred to fairies or spirits survived in Irish folklore into the twentieth century.[14]

Bruidhean Chaoirthainn also offers other clues as to how such a connection may have come about. The narrative revolves around the

Isolated trees or *bile*, especially hawthorn and rowan, have long been seen as sacred to otherworld beings in Ireland.

elements of fire and blood. Both are strongly associated with the colour red. Fire and blood are woven through the tale like a crimson thread, ravelled out from that first signal appearance of the rowan's scarlet berries. Fire, the story's chief antagonist, initially offers warmth, the promise of edible meat; blood, shed tragically in battle, later becomes an agent of magical unbinding. Both blood and fire connect the material and spiritual realms through the ritual of sacrifice. Might the rowan's magical qualities, its liminal status, have derived from these ancient symbolic associations operant within the colour red? Certainly, red is a colour associated with otherworldliness across early Irish literature – otherworld cattle have red ears, for example.

The symbolism of fire and blood, however, transcends the pagan context, and the narrative is equally susceptible to Christian interpretations. The shimmering rowan berries outside the almost-fatal hall are redolent of the Christian idea of *vanitas* – the temptation of earthly pleasures, which are empty or spiritually harmful. Rowan is an apt choice for this symbolism, since the berries, though aesthetically appealing, are bitter and unpalatable. The *bruidhean* itself clearly has hellish connotations. If Finn is at risk of damnation, then the ransom blood shed by his chivalric companions has a Christological connection, making the scarlet berries foreshadow a redemptive sacrifice: with

Blackbird feeding on rowan berries. Both birds and the colour red are strongly associated with the otherworld in early Irish literature.

Diarmuid's unflinching bravery, we are entering the realms of Christian chivalry familiar to readers of Arthurian romance.

For now, however, let us remain in the otherworld of speculation, seeking further clues to rowan's significance as a conduit to the realm of spirits. We have noted the importance of colour symbolism here, but might there be additional ecological reasons for the link? One conjecture is that rowan's threshold presence owes something to its association with birds. Rowan berries are of conspicuous edibility to many forms of avian life, and birds, in the Irish tales, are often manifestations of otherworld beings.[15] It is not difficult to see why this should be so: in their itinerant and aerial lives, birds are always slipping out of sight, disappearing for months beyond the known world. Perhaps the rowan, frequently seeded by birds and therefore apt to appear enigmatically in new places, acquired some of the same imaginative associations with otherworldliness. In one tale, Cú Chulainn is informed of an otherworld location where 'three trees of crimson crystal' play host to a magic flock whose singing soothes and heals; it is easy to think of these as dreamily transfigured rowans.[16]

Without doubt, forms of genuine ecological attention are tightly woven into the symbolic landscape of the tales. For example, in 'The Pursuit of Diarmuid and Grainne', a popular saga surviving in a seventeenth-century manuscript, but which is referenced in a list of tales dating back to the ninth century, a magic rowan, 'the quicken tree of Dubhros', grows from a berry dropped by the *Tuatha dé* as they return, aerially, to the occulted otherworld.[17] Though it is not mentioned that the *Tuatha* are in bird form – as they often are in the tales – the image is instantly evocative of such an ecology, suggesting the idea of the rowan as a plant dispersed by otherworldly means and thus retaining a trace of the spirit realm.

The Dubhros rowan can also be connected to the ancient Irish tradition of sacred trees or *bíle*.[18] Its berries have an ambrosial effect, giving youth to whoever eats them. In the episodic story, which tells how Diarmuid is tricked into betraying Finn and bound by oath to elope with Grainne, his master's bride-to-be, the magical rowan

H. J. Ford, 'Diarmid and Grania in the Quicken Tree', illustration from Andrew Laing, ed., *The Book of Romance* (1903). The 19th century saw a remarkable revival of interest in Celtic mythology.

offers sanctuary to the fleeing lovers. Retreating to its branches, they live off the berries until Finn tracks them down. The tree's rejuvenating fruit recalls the image of the otherworld as a place of continuous banqueting and perpetual youth. The notion that gods lived in a state of ageless beauty, a quality preserved by a special spiritual repast, is common to many pagan belief systems, serving as a basis for sacrificial practices in which blood, bearer of life-force, was offered as nourishment.[19] Again, these ideas flicker in the background of the story, the rowan's blood-red berries serving as an aestheticized reminder of archaic practice.

While the Finn tales may offer an enigmatic glimpse into the pagan spirit realm – and rowan's importance in negotiating its boundary – it is unlikely the figure of an Irish shaman would be our first association when thinking of ancient Celtic religion. The popular image of Celtic paganism is dominated by the Druids.

Rowan's connection to an imagined Druidry is strong. At some point, it acquired the colloquial moniker *fid na ndruad* – the Druid's tree.[20] In Geoffrey Keating's seventeenth-century *History of Ireland*, we are told that Druids made 'round wattles of the quicken tree and spread thereon the offered in sacrifice . . . to summon the demons to get information from them'.[21] From this, Keating states, 'The old saw has since been current which says that one has *gone on his wattles of knowledge* when he has done his utmost to obtain information.' A similar idea is present in the hagiographic 'Life of Berach', in which Druids sit on hurdles of rowan wood, drinking a special beer to facilitate prophecy.[22]

While Keating's reference to the Druids presents them as a curiosity, a way of explaining obscure idiom, their presence in earlier texts is far more ideologically loaded. By the start of the eighth century, references to Druids as magico-religious functionaries of pagan society are absent from Irish law, so that it seems the Druid had been defeated.[23] Little direct evidence of their rituals survives. Druids, however, make frequent appearances in early Irish hagiographies and pseudo-historical tales, their confrontation with saints serving as a microcosm of the contest between paganism and Christianity. Such tales are propagandistic caricatures, eliding local events with biblical models: the seventh-century *Life* of St Patrick compares the pagan King Lóegaire and his Druids to the Old Testament Nebuchadnezzar and his magi; Patrick's defeat of the magician Lochru recalls the confrontation of St Peter with Simon Magus in the Acts of the Apostles.[24]

Possibly the most bombastic example of such propaganda is 'The Siege of Knocklong', a text likely dating to the twelfth century and which contains some amazingly over-the-top Druidical rowan magic. At the centre of the tale is the mercurial figure of Mug Ruith, a recurring literary magician who, in a fragmentary text collected in the *Book of Leinster*, is attested to have lived through the reigns of nineteen kings and to have learnt magic directly from the scriptural Simon Magus.[25]

'The Siege' tells of the legendary pseudo-historical King Cormac mac Airt (whose reign is dated by saga writers to the third century) as he attempts to impose a taxation of cattle on Munster. When the Munstermen decide to fight this claim, Cormac embarks on a bitter campaign to extort payment. Desperate, the Munster side turn to the blind elderly Mug Ruith for help. Protracted warfare culminates in the lurid description of a devastating Druidic fire, which Mug conjures with a series of sinister incantations:

> I knead a fire, powerful, strong;
> it will level the wood, it will dry up grass;
> an angry flame, great its speed
> it will rush up, to the heavens above;
> . . .
> God of druids,
> my god above every god,
> he is god of the ancient druids
> it will blow (the wind), may it blow
> a low flame (to burn) the young vegetation,
> a high flame for the old (vegetation),
> a quick burning of the old,
> a quick burning of the new,
> sharp smoke of the rowan-tree,
> gentle smoke of the rowan-tree,
> I practise druidic arts,
> I subdue Cormac's power.[26]

Stirred by these exhortations, Mug's rowan-stoked blaze burns out of control, consuming the forests of Munster. Meanwhile, he summons a blood rain to horrify Cormac's army, flying among the clouds in a mask of feathers as he fans the flames from above.

According to toponymic lore, the druid Mide lit a fire on the Hill of Uisneach, which burned for seven years. Geoffrey Keating reported that May Day or Beltane fires, often of rowan wood, still burned there in the 17th century.

Exploiting the rowan's familiar symbological connection with fire and blood, 'The Siege' is a triumph of schlocky apocalyptic atmosphere. In Irish tradition, Mug Ruith was often connected with Simon Magus, a figure seen by Christians as an archetype for the temptation of heresy; some early poems even make Mug responsible for beheading John the Baptist.[27] Mug's presence in the tale, therefore, acts as a bridge to biblical time; implying a powerful sense of continuity between the history of Ireland and the world of scripture, it allows the author to reimage the pagan Druids as practitioners of an organized satanic monotheism – an apocalyptic anti-Christianity. By creating an antagonist of such biblical grandeur, 'The Siege' elevates the drama of Irish conversion to the level of spiritual archetype, an ageless drama of good and evil – and it places rowan at its centre.

A more subtle handling of rowan's Druidic associations can be found in the early saga 'The Wooing of Étaín'. When Étaín, the dazzlingly beautiful daughter of an Ulster king, is chosen as a bride by the semi-divine Midir, his existing wife, Fúamnach, fostered by a Druid, is unsurprisingly jealous. The description of the curse she lays on Étaín, using a 'wand of scarlet rowan', is a virtuoso performance, vivid concreteness sliding off into profound enigma:

Étaín sat in the chair in the centre of the house, whereupon Fúamnach struck her with a wand of scarlet rowan and turned her into a pool of water. Fúamnach went to her foster-father Bresal [the Druid], then, and Mider left the house to the water that had been made of Étaín . . . The heat of the fire and the air and the seething of the ground combined to turn the pool of water . . . into a worm, and . . . the worm into a scarlet fly. This fly was the size of the head of the handsomest man in the land, and the sound of its voice and the beating of its wings were sweeter than pipes and harps and horns. Its eyes shone like precious stones in the dark, and its colour and fragrance could sate hunger and quench thirst in any man; moreover, a sprinkling of the drops it shed from its wings could cure every sickness and affliction in the land.[28]

Perhaps most indicative of our distance from the imaginative world of these stories is the choice of a fly for Étaín's final form. Some translators have sought to mitigate its impact by suggesting that a butterfly was meant.[29] Yet, there is no indication of this in the language used, and to import a more charismatic insect into the story is to refuse what seems the most startling claim made by the text: that there is spiritual nourishment in attention to every aspect of the created world, even something as insignificant as a fly – 'its colour and fragrance could sate hunger.' Throughout the passage, I'd suggest, the author argues for a subtle transvaluation of values, mischievously juxtaposing the trappings of earthly wealth with the minutiae of nature. When we look aright, a fly's eyes can be bright as gemstones, the buzzing of its wings sweeter than music. Patterns of metamorphosis – water, worm, fly – evoke a genuine ecological astonishment: there is wonder, the story insists, in how the elements somehow conspire in miraculous teeming life. The passage quoted alludes to Genesis – 'let the waters bring forth abundantly the moving creatures that have life' – so that the fly's appearance embodies the idea of spontaneous generation in nature, a manifestation of divine involvement in everything that is and shall be.[30] Relating Étaín's rebirth, the anonymous author deliberately pits the quiet magic of creation against the showy pagan spells symbolized in the work of Fúamnach's Druidical rowan wand.

The rowan thus assumes a rich and multifaceted significance. While still connected to dangerous pagan dabblings, it is also celebrated as part of a vision of natural beauty, an emblem of a deeper, more powerful mystery. By designating it 'scarlet', the author reminds us of the vivid colour of the rowan's berries – an aesthetic appeal best

Stephen Reid, 'Midir and Étaín', illustration from T. W. Rolleston, *Myths and Legends: The Celtic Race* (1910).

'What's red is beautiful', detail from the Book of Kells, 9th century, showing the opening of St John's gospel.

summed up by the words of Cú Chulainn's wife, Emer, in another tale: 'What's red is beautiful.'[31] And while the harmful wand is red, the healing fly, too, is within that colour range. This chromatic resonance allows the wand to be momentarily recontextualized as part of the ecology of living rowan – to reclaim its part in the natural splendour celebrated by the scene.

In Étaín's story, then, we glimpse a far more positive idea of rowan. In many Irish texts, the tree's appeal is highlighted by its use in conventional literary blazons – the celebratory description of personal beauty in a catalogue of anatomical features. Most familiar from subsequent literature are those describing ideal female beauty. A typical example is this description of Étaín: 'White of the snow of one night were the two hands, soft and even, and red as a foxglove were the two clear-beautiful cheeks . . . Blue as a hyacinth were the eyes. Red as rowan-berries the lips.'[32]

More surprising to modern readers are those blazons celebrating male beauty. In 'Cormac's Adventure in the Land of Promise', a saga collected in the fourteenth-century *Book of Ballymote*, but likely written around 1200, the author describes a 'great meeting' at Tara held in the time of Cormac mac Airt.[33] At this colloquy, crucial legal questions

Earthworks at the Hill of Tara, County Meath, usually identified as the centre of early Irish high kingship. The earthwork on the right is known as *Teach Chormaic*, Cormac's House.

are decided. In keeping with the theme of idealized sovereignty – the tale celebrates a time of 'peace and ease and happiness', an era of perfect order 'full of every good thing' – the description of the High King is a vision of exceptional splendour:

> Splendidly did Cormac enter the great meeting . . . his like in beauty had never come . . . He was shapely . . . without blemish, without disgrace. Thou wouldst deem a shower of pearls had been cast into his head. Thou wouldst deem that his mouth was a cluster of rowan-berries. Whiter than snow was his nobly built body. His cheek was like . . . a mountain-foxglove. Like blue-bells were his eyes.[34]

While, in Étaín's blazon, the invocation of rowan is limited to a conventional chromatic index, here the author luxuriates in the sensuous materiality of the image: in an unexpected twist, Cormac's mouth becomes a 'cluster of rowan-berries', suggesting an almost erotic fixation on texture and palpable fleshiness. Indeed, the author seems to value the berries not just for their colour, which is so obvious as to need no explicit mention, but for their materialization of abundance: presiding over a time of 'mast and fatness and sea-produce', Cormac becomes a kingly embodiment of the fertility of the land when governed according to principles of equity, justice and order.

Cormac's blazon is typical of the idealized presentation of Irish High Kings, especially the mythical monarchs of the deep past, and its imagery implies a characteristically Irish synthesis of pagan and Christian elements. For many scholars, the pagan High Kings of Ireland, at least as retrospectively portrayed in the literature, can be seen as 'sacral' rulers – monarchs ritually married to the land as a personified goddess.[35] In Cormac's person, this occult union is figuratively present in the blazon, which imaginatively marries the king's mortal person to the fecund beauty of Irish nature: Cormac's radiant androgyny is suffused with this doubling, as his mortal male body shimmers with divine femininity – a mystical event in which the rowan, emblem of plenty and female fertility, plays a crucial mediating role.

The symbolism of rowan here is more complex still, however. For while gesturing to pagan traditions, the author also contains them within a highly unorthodox Christian framework. To appreciate this fully, we have to skip to the end of the story, where we find that Cormac's unprecedented sovereign judgement derives from a magical cup, a gift from one of the enigmatic *Tuatha dé*, the godly otherworld being Manannan. The figure of Manannan, most scholars agree, likely derived from the lore of a pagan deity. In handling such figures, Christian writers had to take care, with two dependably orthodox narrative strategies available to them: either the old gods could be re-framed as devils, or they could be presented as heroic rulers from the past who had been gradually deified by ancestral superstitions. Irish storytellers, however, and especially the earliest writers, seem to have daringly rejected these accepted narrative options: in Cormac's tale, Manannan is an agent of undoubted benevolence; he is also clearly not human.[36]

Indeed, rather than demonizing the gods of their mythical fore-bears (and celebrating the spiritual struggle to overcome paganism), many Irish writers preferred to tell a different, riskier story. Depicting their homeland as a place haunted by semi-divine 'god-peoples' (*Tuatha dé*), they presented these mysterious beings, Manannan included, either as 'half-fallen' angels or as a race of humans who had somehow avoided the Fall: untainted by original sin, these beings preserved a trace of Adam's initial perfection, of human nature as originally created by God.[37] All agreed, however, that at some point in time the *Tuatha dé* had retreated from the mortal world, living in hollow mounds (or *síde*) and fleeing to islands within bodies of water and across the sea.

In early stories such as 'The Voyage of Bran' or the 'The Adventure of Connlae', an encounter with the *Tuatha dé* is depicted as an angelic visitation which initiates a journey of spiritual purification.[38] The tale of Cormac's wisdom explicitly references this tradition: 'the wise declare that whenever any strange apparition was revealed of old to the royal lords . . . as the Land of Promise was shewn to Cormac – it was a divine ministration . . . and not a demoniacal ministration . . .

In the narrative imagination of the early Irish tales, a cluster of rowan berries can be a mystical symbol of fertility.

Rowans by the Neolithic passage tomb at Newgrange. In early Irish literature,
such burial mounds often figure as homes to the mysterious *Tuatha dé*.

for they followed Natural Truth, and they served the commandment
of the Law'.[39] Cormac himself is described as 'without blemish, without
disgrace', a detail that adds a theological dimension to his perfection
as a sovereign, presenting him as free from original sin.[40]

Such background affords deeper insight into the intertextual richness and theological complexity of the idealized description of King
Cormac – and rowan's symbolic place in it. In describing the king as
'without blemish' – a phrase used in other tales to describe the *Tuatha
dé* themselves – the author gestures to the heretical notion that, despite
the Fall, their pagan forebears were able to attain an Adamic natural
perfection through the institution of just laws. Cormac's wisdom,
emblemized by Manannan's cup, is a gift from the benign otherworld
of the *Tuatha dé*; the Ireland he presides over becomes an image of that
alternate reality. At first sight conventional and straightforward, the
blazon that describes King Cormac then places its 'cluster of rowan
berries' at the centre of a political-theological vision of considerable
intricacy. Through the contrivance of metaphor, a figure that bridges

presence and absence, the writer transforms familiar aspects of the landscape into fragments of an unfallen existence, saturating the beauteous person of the king with a mystical vision of an Irish Eden. In a landscape made pregnant with occulted spiritual depth, something as simple as a cluster of rowan berries can be a mystic symbol of natural perfection.[41]

'The Cattle Raid of Fróech', which may date to the eighth century, also finds rowan mediating between a vision of adonic male beauty and the allure of an angelic otherworld. In this tale, the semi-divine hero Fróech travels to the court of King Ailill and Queen Medb to win their daughter Findabair's hand in marriage. Findabair desires the match, and Fróech is a worthy suitor. However, when Ailill names what he deems an extravagant bride-price, Fróech refuses to negotiate and storms off. Ailill and Medb become anxious that Findabair and Fróech will elope. In a bid to get rid of the problem, Ailill deliberately exposes Fróech to mortal danger, asking him to swim across a stream for a berried sprig of rowan. He neglects to mention that the river's depths conceal a fearsome serpent.

The plan, however, backfires. Not only does Fróech survive, but the vision of his body in the water, its graceful radiance accented by the rowan branch, strengthens Findabair's desire. It is rendered with gorgeous clarity:

> Fróech made to leave the water. 'Do not come out,' said Ailill, 'until you have brought me a branch from yonder rowan on the river bank. I find its berries beautiful.' Fróech went back, then, and brought the branch through the water on his shoulders. Findabair said afterwards that, whatever beautiful thing she saw, she thought it more beautiful to look at Fróech across the dark water, his body very white, his hair very beautiful, his face very shapely, his eyes very blue, he a gentle youth without fault or blemish, his face narrow below and broad above . . . the branch with the red berries between his throat and his white face.[42]

Again, the hero's body is pointedly described as 'without fault or blemish'. The picture is saturated with the glamour of a sinless otherworld – to which bodies of water often represent a threshold. The colour terms used to describe Fróech are of particular importance here, helping us grasp the force of the rowan's redness as it participates in the symbolic assemblage. First, there is the enigmatic Old Irish *glas*, used to describe Fróech's eyes. Translated in the above version as 'blue', it has connotations of dazzle and translucency, the dynamic play of sky reflected in water – all indicators of theophanic presence. In hagiography, the colour is associated with martyrdom and with spiritual ordeals such as praying while submerged in water.[43] Added to this, there is the whiteness of Fróech's body. The word used in the Irish version is *gel*, a non-basic term indicating a dazzling or brilliant white.[44] Perhaps its closest equivalent is the Latin *candidus*, used by Christian authors to describe the pristine robes donned by the recently baptized – robes which themselves symbolized the body cleansed of any sin or shame and returned to Adamic perfection.[45] Finally, the scene's triadic juxtaposition of black, white and red recalls a widespread folk motif, which may connect these later religious meanings with archaic notions of the sacred.[46]

Again, the rowan plays its part in a symbolic framework of considerable sophistication. Narrative elements likely dating back to oral stories, as well as pagan sovereignty motifs, are layered with overtly Christian resonances. A kind of baptism, Fróech's ordeal in the pool represents a rebirth from sin, present in the obvious shape of the water-serpent whose head he strikes off. As well as connoting otherworldly beauty, then, the rowan berries may again be intended as a reminder of Christ's blood, shed to absolve humans from the Fall.

The idea of this aquatic trial as a spiritual rebirth also helps explain an element of the story sometimes attributed to a confusion between different oral sources. For after his narrow escape from the pool, Fróech is taken by the women of the otherworld who arrive weeping and lamenting as if the hero had died. While there, he is 'completely healed, without fault or blemish' and returns 'as if he had come from another world'. Rather than preserving a trace of an older story in which the hero is killed by the monster, Fróech's 'death' may allegorize the Christian theme of baptism as participation in Christ's crucifixion, a theme explained by St Paul (Romans 6.4): 'we are buried with him by baptism into death that like as Christ was raised up from the dead . . . even so we also should walk in newness of life'. In Fróech's story, the rowan, too, is given 'newness of life'; shimmering with layered associations, it is central to the complex reanimation of a familiar narrative scene.

Though the old religion had been quelled in Ireland by the seventh century, the spectre of paganism was not long settled. From the end of the eighth century, Viking raids became a source of urgent concern, and by the ninth century, the Norsemen had permanent settlements in Dublin and along the eastern seaboard.[47] The effect of this close cultural contact on the development of Irish and Norse literature, myth and belief is hard to unpick. Some scholars argue that the prominence of rowan in medieval Irish texts is a direct reflection of Scandinavian influence, its (often-negative) association with pagan magic a reaction to its veneration by the Vikings.[48] For others, only Irish influence can explain the most striking appearance of rowan in the medieval Norse literature – in the famous *Edda*, written by Snorri Sturluson, a Christian scholar living in thirteenth-century Iceland, where it is described as the 'saviour of Thor'.

Though the *Edda* is now the greatest single compendium of Norse mythology we have, it was not written with that intent. Snorri's goal was to educate his readers in the appreciation of skaldic poetry, the elaborate court verses of the old Scandinavian world.[49] Passing into archaism, they were at risk of being forgotten. Skaldic texts are full of elaborate epithets called kennings, common nouns replaced by riddling formulae. A simple example would be something like 'raven-wine' for blood, but often kennings are more elaborate, requiring knowledge of mythology – blood is also 'the river of Fenrir'.

Thor's salvation is a rowan: Lorenz Frølich, 'Thor's Journey to Gierrodsgard', illustration from Viktor Rydberg, *Teutonic Mythology* (1906).

Happily for modern scholars, Snorri's handbook on kennings quotes passages from a number of skaldic poems and, in explicating them, Snorri offers summaries of a range of Norse myths. The story involving rowan explains why Thor is sometimes referred to as 'the giant of Vimur's ford'. Thor, Snorri reminds us, was crossing the Vimur on his way to confront the giant Geirrod, when he was threatened by the river's rapidly rising waters. Peering upstream, he saw that 'Geirrod's daughter Gjalp, [was] standing astride the river . . . causing it to rise.'[50] Managing to dam the flow with a well-aimed stone, the god 'grasp[ed] a sort of rowan-bush and thus climbed out of the river. Hence comes the saying that Thor's salvation is a rowan.'[51]

Much about the episode is enigmatic; no other reference to 'the saying', apparently idiomatic, has been found. Interpreting its meaning, and rowan's meaning in it, is also complicated by the fact that Snorri's version of the story relies on an earlier telling – the skaldic poem *Þórsdrápa* (Poem about Thor), composed by Eilífr Goðrúnarson in the tenth century. Little is known of Eilífr's life, but his writing coincided with a period of intense political turbulence in Norway. He likely frequented the court of Jarl Hákon, a ruler who sponsored a vigorous backlash against the incursion of Christian beliefs and strengthened pagan sovereignty cults.[52] *Þórsdrápa* is the only extant poem to tell a single narrative tale in the highly allusive and metrically intricate style of the skalds, a fact that likely explains the notorious difficulty of its kennings. Thor's arrival at the river, for example, is compressed into a truly head-spinning phrase: 'the heaven-targe-dwelling's blood of the women of Frid's first defiler was reached.'[53] The 'heaven-targe' is the Sun; its dwelling is the sky; sky's blood is water; and 'Frid's first defiler' means a giant. In translation: *Thor reached the giant's water* – the River Vimur.

Because of the compression of this version, scholars have had a hard time deciding whether we are supposed to understand the narrative presence of the giantess Gjalp as literal or whether the story participates in a tradition of referring to landscape features as formed from the bodies of giants, a sort of chthonic animism. It is up for debate, too, whether the strengthened flow of the river is caused by Gjalp's urine or by her menstrual blood. Some have even wondered whether any of the poem's kennings can explain the 'rowan-bush' that features in Snorri's version.[54]

How then, are we to understand the tale? A mythological approach, reading the story for its disclosure of archaic cosmology and beliefs, might see Thor's exploits as preserving the idea of a battle between the gods and older, chthonic deities – representative of dangerous natural forces.[55] Thor's victory over Gjalp and her father, Geirrod, would thus encode the age-old agriculturalist burden of cultivating wild land, a theme that would have continued to resonate with many Norsemen, especially those who had endured their own dangerous crossings to Iceland and beyond. More speculatively, it is possible to see the figure of a menstruating Gjalp as preserving some trace of an older matriarchal religion, a cult in which menses was a source of prophetic wisdom and spiritual power for female shamans.[56] If we understand the story this way, then rowan figures in it as an emblem of tamed femininity, prefiguring the tree's frequent later associations with domesticity.

It is also worth considering the story in relation to religion. During the time of Eilífr's version, Norway was in transition, Christian and pagan beliefs existing in syncretic tension. Though Jarl Hákon attempted to bolster his legitimacy by reinvigorating cult activity, many were converted or adopted elements of Christianity within a polytheistic framework. Thor's cult was particularly susceptible to symbolic appropriations. The possession of Thor's hammer icons seems to have been popular during this period, likely as a reaction to the powerful iconography of the cross, but perhaps also as a non-orthodox Christian symbol in its own right. Early Norse imaginings of Christ often drew on cultural values embodied in Thor – strength, integrity, heroism – and some scholars have seen Eilífr's poem as participating in this syncretistic characterization: Thor's journey in the poem arguably borrows elements from Christ's harrowing of hell; the god is referred to in one kenning as the 'helper of men', an unusual epithet also applied elsewhere to Christ.[57]

Might the poet have sensed that Thor's social and psychological role was being superseded by the arrival of Christ – the old god

A traditional turf church in Iceland, flanked by rowan and yew. Rowan is one of Iceland's few native trees.

somehow both abolished *and* saved by the coming deity? Did he deliberately hedge his own allegiances with a text of riddling ambiguity? Since he was sensitive to such complexities, might we see the accentuated place of rowan in Snorri's version as attempting to draw out religious resonances in Eilífr's telling? As we've seen, the rowan, by virtue of its red berries, can be connected with Christ's blood. Snorri was fond of the euhemerist strategy of explaining the myths of the pagan gods as being derived from stories about charismatic rulers of the past. If Thor were mortal, then, for Snorri, it would be literally true to say that Christ would be 'the saviour of Thor'. On the other hand, as a focus for superstition, and as a source of protection against dangerous natural forces, the rowan might have 'saved Thor' in the sense of maintaining the god's practical function in the midst of conversion. They are intriguing but answerless possibilities.

Whatever Snorri's intentions, rowan's association with Christianity is certainly attested elsewhere in Icelandic literature. In 'The Tale of Geirmund Heljarskin', from the *Sturlunga Saga*, a pagan settler in Iceland is troubled by a strange light that issues from a rowan: 'There's one place on that slope', he explains, 'where, whenever I look at it, the light so blazes into my eyes that I become very uneasy. And the light is always just above the rowan-tree which grows by itself under the lip of the slope.'[58] The rowan, we are later informed by narrative interjection, stood on 'that very place where the church at Skarð now stands'.[59] By proffering this detail, the writer encourages us to read the episode as a proleptic vision of Christianity. Again, the rowan, both wrapped up in old superstitions and the focus of a new illuminating spirit, is a threshold between worlds.

While some scholars sense an Irish influence on Snorri's storytelling, others have heard echoes from another sphere of Norse influence and interchange: the Uralic-language regions of present-day Finland and the Baltic. A thunder god, similar to Thor, exists in the linked religious traditions of both the northern Sámi and the Finns: *Hora galles*, in Sámi religion, is apparently a direct loan from an Old Norse expression meaning 'old man Thor'; the thunder god of the Karelian Finns was known as 'Ukko', the old man. Crucially, in both cases, this god has a wife or consort whose name, Ravdna or Rauni, may be etymologically related to the rowan tree.[60] Might the idea of the thunder god married to a female rowan deity have been taken up by settlers in Iceland, a place where rowan is one of the only native tree species, later informing the 'saviour of Thor' idiom?

Little in the way of written myth concerning Rauni has survived. However, the Finnish *Kalevala*, an episodic poem compiled by the folklorist Elias Lönnrot from oral material collected in nineteenth-century Finnish Karelia, contains abundant evidence of the rowan's sacred and magical aura in the region. Its account of creation, for example, contains a list of trees in which rowan occupies a conspicuous place:

> On lowlands he sowed birches
> Alders in light soils
> . . .
> rowans on holy ground [61]

In a subsequent episode, a rowan fire is used to predict the intentions of strangers approaching by sea:

> Put rowan twigs on the fire
> The choice wood in the flame!
> If it oozes blood
> Then war is coming;
> But if it oozes water
> We'll live on in peace.[62]

As it happens, this particular rowan oozes neither blood nor water, but a honey-like alcoholic spirit. The delegation is a marriage party and their arrival leads to a wedding. After the feast, the bride is given extensive advice on how to act as a wife, a primer in domestic economy. Again, the rowan has its place:

> Be very wary of those
> Rowans in the yard: holy
> Are the rowans in the yard
> Holy are the rowans' boughs
> Holy the boughs' foliage
> The berries still holier
> With which a maid is advised
> . . .
> What pleases a husband
> What touches a bridegroom's heart.[63]

What is meant by this warning? The answer surely hinges around the figural use of the rowan berries as a living symbol of 'what pleases a husband'. The bride is to be 'wary' – or mindful – of the 'holy' rowan because its abundant blood-red fruits encode social expectations of female beauty and fertility. The tree, that is, has been made to sanctify a domestic economy centred around reproduction and the satisfaction of male desire.

Alongside the mythic actions of gods and heroes, these Finnish stories bring us close to the reality of life in a peasant society. Their vision of the sacred is necessarily conservative. For them, holiness comes back to the preservation of order and the maintenance of practices long established by custom: tied to survival, the holy consists in respect for boundaries and the proper observation of seasonal rituals. In this respect, such stories reveal something important about their more fantastical counterparts: the deeper origins of myth and magic in the needs of people living close to the level of subsistence. They ask us to consider how the magical and sacred status of rowan relates to perhaps *the* central question of human survival and flourishing: how to organize social relations of reproduction and fertility,

Janis Rozentāls, *Under the Rowan Tree*, 1905, oil on canvas. The painting encapsulates the strong association between rowan and idealized motherhood in the Baltic region.

both in terms of human kinship and the relationship between human communities and nature.

We get a glimpse of such social questions in the Norse and Irish myths, of course. Behind the idealized presentation of the sovereign, for example, there lies the idea of a political order founded in respect for the fruits of land and sea; Thor's skirmishes with the giants may well concern the domestication of natural forces. But in the literary myths, these issues are seen from the top down. The Finnish tales collected by Lönnrot seem to reverse the priorities, bringing the mythic imagination closer to home. In the next chapter, we will get closer still: for it is on the trail of rowan's historic involvement in negotiations of kinship and survival, as evidenced in folklore, superstition and ritual, that we are about to embark.

two

Magic and Medicine

❧

I n 1551, writing in what is now Finland, but was then part of
Sweden, Mikael Agricola, a Lutheran priest, translated the Psalms
into Finnish for the first time. Having travelled widely in the
region's most rugged outposts, Agricola prefaced the volume with a
description of religion among the Finns. He wasn't impressed. Though
they had long been exposed to Christian influence, both from Sweden
and Russia, Agricola described the peasantry as living in a state of confused semi-conversion.[1] The rural people, he informed his audience,
worshipped 'many false gods'; they held festivals in which 'shameful
deeds were done' and, worst of all, 'in place of God' they 'bowed . . . in
public and private' to 'objects of nature without number'.[2] The only
explanation, he opined, was that they had been led astray by the Devil.

We are fortunate that Agricola, despite his pious horror, was also
sufficiently intrigued by popular religion to record its rituals in some
detail. The earliest written account of the region's folkloric customs,
Agricola's preface includes a rare reference to Rauni – a deity who,
as we saw in the previous chapter, has long been associated with the
rowan tree and considered a wife of the Finnish thunder god, Ukko.
'When the spring sowing was done', Agricola tells us, the people
'drank Ukko's cup' and 'all were drunken', the most auspicious time
for such a ritual being 'when Rauni, Ukko's woman began to splash'
and Ukko had responded with 'great rain from the north'.[3]

The precise meaning of Agricola's language has long been a subject of debate. What does it mean for Rauni 'to splash'? And how does

this relate to the subsequent rains? One answer, assuming Rauni to be a goddess manifested in the rowan, is that the 'splash' is a metaphor for the tree's white blossom. The timing of Ukko's libation would therefore encode an intuitive climatological understanding, that rains most benefit newly sown grain just as the flowers begin to 'splash' on Finland's rowans.

Assuming a ritual symbolism closely motivated by ecological attention and the imaginative use of analogy, such an interpretation offers a compelling sense of the tight connection between the development

John Savio, *Rowan, Lofoten*, 1928–34, woodcut. A Sami artist from northern Norway, Savio's woodcut references the rowan's connection to a northern thunder god.

A 'splash' of blossom on *Sorbus aucuparia.*

of folk religion and the urgent concerns of agricultural communities. In the ritual imagination of the Finns, the seasonal correspondence of flowering rowans with spring rains is transformed into a cipher for divine marriage: with its white bouquets of spring blossom, the tree is easily figured as a virginal bride; seen against snow, its blood-red berries, lingering deep into winter, become a sign of the fruitful consummation of celestial and earthly energies. The persistence of these gendered associations between rowan and fertility, both natural and social, is evinced in riddles collected by later folklorists: 'A rowan on a sacred hill, a sacred leaf on the rowan. – A bride.'[4]

Devoted to the folklore of rowan, this chapter explores the tree's role in the obscure lives of people such as Agricola's nameless Karelian peasants – people who eked out a tough and precarious existence in Europe's northern latitudes: in Ireland, Scotland, upland regions of England and Wales, Scandinavia, the Baltic and northern Russia. These are places where the growing season is short and at the mercy of unpredictable weather; where wild animals, such as bears and wolves, may threaten precious grazing animals; where the ground is rugged, boggy and mountainous – where rowan thrives.

In the course of our journey, we'll find rowan used in seasonal fertility rituals but also in rites for the protection and blessing of

Finnish postage
stamp from 1972,
illustrating historic
female dress from
the Perniö region
and the symbolic
association of rowan
with idealized
femininity.

livestock and, especially, as an apotropaic against witchcraft and
malicious or mischievous spirits. Most of all, in delving into the beliefs,
customs and practices of people often forgotten and misunderstood
by history, we'll have a chance to consider the ingenuity of the human
imagination – especially under conditions of fragility and hardship
– in places where the boundaries of self and society are dangerously
susceptible to penetration by the wild.

As evidence of 'folk religion', Agricola's preface is something of an
anomaly.[5] It seems to offer a glimpse of a genuine 'pagan survival' –
an organized religious observance tied to a well-defined polytheistic
faith and from which we can glean a coherent sense of ritual symbolism. It was once commonplace to see *all* popular superstition
as evidence for the persistence of paganism among an uneducated
and irrational peasantry – to believe that Christianity had only ever
been present among them as a thin 'veneer'.[6] Peasant culture, it is true,
often confronts us with a confusing muddle of ideas: lines are blurred
between magic and ritual; saints, angels and demons coexist with entities such as fairies, elves and nature spirits. Yet most of those con-
versant in such lore would not have hesitated to identify themselves
as Christian, and the vast majority of evidence for folk belief comes
from societies long converted to Christianity.[7]

Scholars, by and large, now see the notion of 'pagan survivals' as rather patronizing, obscuring the complexity and dynamism of vernacular religious culture as a distinctive social form.[8] Such richness is abundantly evident in one of the most intriguing documents of life in pre-Norman England – and one of the few to mention the *cwic-beam* or rowan: the text of the 'Field Blessing Ceremony', or *Æcerbot*, a West Saxon metrical charm known from a single eleventh-century manuscript.[9] Describing a ritual for the reinvigoration of unproductive

Beda Stjernschantz, *Pastoraali*, 1897, oil on canvas. In this Finnish symbolist painting, the rowan, just starting to blossom, is associated with purity and fertility.

land, the field blessing offers vivid insight into the quasi-magical services provided by the early Christian Church, as well as its ability to assimilate customs likely derived from native religions.[10] It may also have been related to the more widespread and better known Rogation Day ritual of beating the parish bounds, tracing the edges of communal land and asking for protection and fertility.

The broad outline of the rite is fairly simple: the farmer presented four bits of earth, dug from each corner of the degraded field, to the local priest; these would be sanctified by four masses and then returned to the land. After a few more ritual performances, fertility would hopefully be restored. The details, however, are staggeringly involved. First of all, before delivery to the church, each sod had to be anointed with a preparatory array of natural substances: oil, honey, yeast and milk; twigs from all the farm's trees; herbs and holy water. Moreover – and it is here that rowan played its decisive role – while the priest was busy with the four masses, the farmer was advised to make four crosses of *cwic-beam*, inscribe them with the names of the evangelists ('Matheus ond Marcus, Lucas ond Johannes') and place them in the holes where the earth had been dug. Finally, when the turves were returned, an even more bewildering set of prostrations, prayers and invocations was completed, including an intricate blessing of the plough and a beautiful, mysterious address to 'Erce, erce, erce, earth's mother'. In this second phase of the ritual, it is even stipulated that

Jules Breton, *The Blessing of Wheat in Artois*, 1857, oil on canvas. The Christian Church's involvement with rites of agricultural fertility has a long history in Europe.

the petitioner must exchange seed with an itinerant almsman, giving away twice what he received – a detail that implies the ceremony had a wider social context, being performed seasonally throughout the kingdom.[11] The redistributive aspect of the rite would have helped diversify sown seed, assisting farmers in selecting strains that grew most effectively in a particular area.[12]

As with any text so rare, complex and suggestive, there are many ways of interpreting this ritual and the rowan's role in its ceremonial economy. If we want to look for underlying pagan frameworks beneath the ostensibly Christian surface, we might begin by noting certain parallels with the Finnish rite so scathingly observed by Agricola. Both involve the rowan at the charged moment of spring sowing; the pouring of holy water over the prepared turves is reminiscent of the Finns' desire for 'great rains' to promote a lavish growth of grain. If we recall, too, the enigmatic connection of rowan with the thunder god, Thor, of Germanic paganisms, then the parallels become even more tantalizing. Might rowan have been specifically stipulated in the rite because of its ability to designate the farmed soil as the sky god's bride?[13] Certainly, the ritual retains some structural suggestion of a conciliation between earthly and celestial powers: it invokes, in turn, the 'holy guardian of the heavenly kingdom' and the 'mother of earth' – with the latter implored to 'grow pregnant in the embrace of God, filled with food for mortals' use'.[14]

But to state with certainty that such imagery was derived from archaic Germanic religion is impossible, especially since other explanations are equally plausible. Equating God with a masculine celestial force, while personifying Earth as feminine matter, *Æcerbot* exhibits a gendered logic with an ancient philosophical pedigree, framing the spring sowing as a seasonal repetition of the original miracle of Creation.[15] Much of the detail of the charm can be interpreted through a scriptural lens, aligning the purification and blessing of the field with the restoration of Earth to a benevolent Edenic state. The prepared sods, for example, act as both a microcosm of the world and as an emblem of Adam as the first created human: in the apocryphal tradition, the first man, representing humankind in a state of perfection, was created from soil drawn from the four corners of the earth.[16]

Seen this way the field blessing integrated pressing economic concerns with the ideal of social harmony guarded by the Church, combining the powerful Christian fantasy of a return to Eden with the mystery of redemption through Christ's sacrifice.[17] The burial of rowan crosses as a hinge point in the whole process seems especially apt, organizing the urgent matter of agricultural fertility – the livelihood of the entire community – around the central Christian narrative of death and resurrection. But why these crosses should be made specifically of rowan remains enigmatic. Is the specification a remnant of older beliefs? Or does it offer evidence of a very old but also rather mercurial association of the tree with Christ – an association that, in this case, seems to map Christian spiritual meanings backwards onto pre-existing connections of the tree with fertility and life-force?[18] There is much that we can never know.

Though it seeks efficacy on an almost cosmic scale, the field-blessing ceremony is also a straightforward rite of healing and protection, a ritual directly comparable to folk procedures with more local or specialized concerns. A short preface to the ceremony tells us, in fact, that it may be used for land 'if any harm has been done . . . by sorcery or by witchcraft'; its closing invocations beg protection against 'every harm from witchcraft sown throughout the land'.[19]

In succeeding centuries, rowan's use in such counter-magical protection would emerge as the best-known and most widespread of its folkloric associations. Unlike the *Æcerbot* ceremony, in which the counter-magical procedure took place under the auspices of the church, most counter-magical and healing uses of rowan would have been the preserve, either of ordinary people in their everyday life or of those specialized practitioners known in Britain as 'cunning folk' – individuals whose services ranged from exorcism to the location of stolen goods, from identifying the source of magical or spiritual harm to divination and the making of charms.

Since the earliest conversions, most official churches have viewed any ritual act claiming magical efficacy as *a priori* heretical. As a seventeenth-century English writer observed, many would technically 'become witches, by endeavouring to defend themselves against witch-craft': from the most unforgivingly rigorous elite perspective, a rowan amulet placed against witchcraft was itself a devilish dabbling.[20] In practice, however, the spiritually ambiguous arena of unofficial magic was often left to function relatively undisturbed among the peasantry. In societies that lacked effective medicine, and in which countless people lived in fear of random misfortune, it ministered to needs – psychological and practical – that the Church could never fully meet. It was not until the turbulent centuries of the Reformation, in fact, that a concerted effort was made to persecute cunning folk – whom rural people saw as useful 'white witches' – as 'witches' in the malevo-lent sense.[21] As we shall see, much early documentary evidence for popular magical belief in the rowan comes from witchcraft trials and elite writings about witchcraft from that era.

Of the numerous uncertainties and challenges of folk life, perhaps the most devastating and insidious was disease. Though generally not the most prominent ingredient in traditional pharmacology, rowan has its place in remedies that blur the boundaries of the magical and natural. In *Bald's Leechbook*, an Anglo-Saxon medical compendium of the ninth century, we find the bark of *cwic-beam* included in poultices for shingles and scabs. A similar text, *Lacnunga*, specifies that the ingre-dients of a 'bone-salve . . . efficient against head-ache and . . . weakness of all limbs', be stirred with rowan. In this case, the magical significance of the material seems clear, being designed to invest the mixture with the quickening power proper to the tree. Another *Lacnunga* charm, the 'Holy Salve' specifies that the mixing stick be inscribed with the names of the Evangelists and marked with a sign of the cross – as with the field blessing, rowan is pivotal to a healing procedure based on the expulsion of spirits.[22]

Diorama of a 'cunning woman' at the Museum of Witchcraft and Magic,
Boscastle, Cornwall.

Many of the prescriptions of folk medicine invoke the power of
the saints, and many of these saints' legends were likely repositories
for beliefs and functions once performed by pagan gods. A Russian
text of the seventeenth century recounts how 'every year on the Friday
before St Elijah's day' (20 July), peasants and churchmen would come
from the surrounding villages to a certain rowan tree on which an
icon of the saint was hung; they would bring with them icons dedicated to another saint, 'the Holy Martyr Paraskeva', and, on arrival,
they 'prayed to her and lifted babies and small children through the
branches of the rowan'.[23] According to the eminent nineteenth-
century folklorist Alexander Afanasyev, the body's passage through a
split branch of rowan formed into a hoop was a widespread means of
magical healing among the Slavs.[24] In the seventeenth-century example, passage through the tree explicitly designates the rowan as a living
locus for the spiritual power of the saints. It has been speculated, moreover, that Elijah and Paraskeva are Orthodox Christian proxies for
pagan deities, specifically Perun and Mokosh – gods symbolically
correspondent, in the religion of the ancient Slavs, to the powers of
sky and earth, male and female principles of fertility.[25] Perhaps more

than that of any other saint, Paraskeva's cult has seemed to scholars – and disapproving ecclesiastical authorities – to be a focus for pagan survivals, especially associated with feminine nature divinities and their protection of the household. Numerous records exist of her icon being placed in healing or sacred trees (though these were usually birch).[26] The St Elijah's day ritual, therefore, adds to the sense of a widespread pattern of association between rowan and archaic gods in eastern Europe and Russia.

The connection to a thunder god may also explain another well-attested magical use of rowan: as a protection against lightning strikes. The use of rowan wreathes or twigs hung in the eaves of houses and barns to ward off storm damage is recorded from Germany, Scandinavia, the Baltic and Russia.[27] Afanasyev considered the apotropaic and healing powers of rowan to be derived from its status as a visual metaphor for lightning – the red colour of the berries symbolic of celestial fire. When rowan is used to guard against lightning, it works by mimetic appropriation; when used, as it once was in Sweden and Germany, to encourage milk production in cows, a rowan switch is charged with the quickening force of the thunderbolt.[28] Alternatively, oral folklore collected from Estonia implies that rowan's protection against lightning was derived from the pentagram-like shape made by the remnant of calyx at the base of its berries: 'one can stand under a rowan tree . . . because their berries have crosses.'[29] Rather than offering direct protection against lightning, the rowan ensured a safe distance from the Devil, the lightning's true target – 'the cross forbids the evil one from coming under . . . the lightning always wants to strike him'.[30] Whatever the precise logic of the belief, such examples offer a window into the ingenuity of the imagination, its capacity to craft a psychic defence against otherwise insoluble problems.

For Afanasyev, it was rowan's metonymic status as an embodiment of lightning, a zagged snapshot of wrathful divine energy, that explained its special power against the Devil – a belief so widespread that it takes us beyond the Slavic, Baltic and Germanic regions to the Celtic edges of the continent. The notion of rowan's power against

Woodcut of St Paraskeva, Bulgaria, 19th century. Some scholars see the saint as a proxy for ancient Slavic nature divinities.

the Devil is sufficiently well reflected in Lithuanian folk tales as to organize plotlines recurrent in traditional lore. These are listed in Stith Thompson's compendious *Motif-Index of Folk-Literature* – an index of the basic storylines of folk tales – as 'the devil is caught with a switch of rowan tree' and 'the devil overpowered with a stick of rowan'. The same belief is recorded from Estonia.[31] At traditional Lithuanian wedding celebrations, the master of ceremonies might carry a stick rattle (*džingulis*) made of rowan wood and decorated with coloured rags and bells. This had a practical purpose, being shaken to announce arrivals or gain attention for dances and ceremonial gift exchange. Since weddings were an open affair at which itinerant and uninvited guests might expect to be offered hospitality, it also had a protective function, ensuring safety from possibly malevolent intrusion.[32]

Though the apotropaic and healing power of rowan likely has pre-Christian origins, it is the development of these ideas into the notion of protection against the Devil that best explains rowan's prominence in relation to witchcraft beliefs. Evidence for this is abundant, but especially dates to the Reformation – an era in which a strong connection between witchcraft and the Devil, including the sensational apparatus of coven and satanic pact, was being outlined by theologians and legal authorities. Rowan was deployed against bewitchment in a number of ways: as a household amulet against curses or the evil-eye, in charms carried on the person to ward off magical harm and in devices used to protect livestock and animal products from magical theft. 'Rown-tree and red thread', a Scottish saying goes, 'will put the witches to their speed.'[33]

One of the earliest written references to such beliefs is to be found in *Daemonologie*, a learned treatise on witchcraft written by James VI of Scotland (later James I of England). Drawing on contemporary continental thought, James takes a hard-line approach to the theoretical identification of witchcraft, condemning as 'the deville's rudimentes' *all* popular magic and medicine: 'all that which is called vulgarly the vertue of worde, herbe, & stone: which is used by unlawful charmes,

'Their berries have crosses': the protective power of rowan has sometimes been explained by the pentagram-like remnant of calyx at the base of the berries.

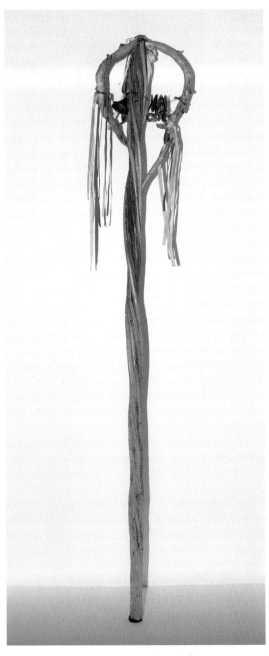

Traditional Lithuanian stick-rattle or *džíngulis* (by Roman Urnižas),
often made of rowan wood to give them a protective function.

Title page of James I's
Daemonologie (1603).

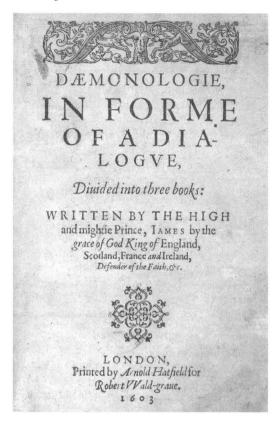

DÆMONOLOGIE,
IN FORME
OF A DIA-
LOGVE,

Diuided into three books:

WRITTEN BY THE HIGH
and mightie Prince, I A M E S by the
grace of God King of England,
Scotland, France *and* Ireland,
Defender of the Faith, &c.

LONDON,
Printed by *Arnold Hatfield* for
Robert VVald-graue.
1 6 0 3

without naturall causes . . . such kinde of Charmes as commonlie
dafte wives use'. He gives as an example the attachment of 'roun-trees
to the haire or tailes' of livestock.[34]

Composed in the 1590s, when James was actively engaged in the
virulent persecution of alleged Scottish witches, the very existence of
the *Daemonologie* is testament to the intimate link between witch hunt-
ing and the extension of state power during the period.[35] Indeed,
James may have seen the hurried publication of the work as a political
necessity, justifying his support for intense campaigns of prosecution
and punishment by presenting witches as a satanic conspiracy against
the divinely licensed authority of church and king. Certainly, this is
the rhetoric richly fleshed out in a play written for James a few years
later: *Macbeth*. One of Shakespeare's most explicated tragedies, it

nevertheless contains a line – 'Aroint thee, witch!' – whose precise linguistic provenance has long puzzled lexicographers and bardologists. In 1874, the editor of a variorum edition of Shakespeare, Horace H. Furness, noted that the phrase bore some similarity to words 'rynt thee' – once spoken by Cheshire milkmaids to their cows. Furness concluded that 'aroint', likely derived from a similar dialect phrase known to Shakespeare, simply meant 'budge' or 'move on'. But the eminent gentleman missed a trick, failing to connect the milkmaids' goading with an origin already put forward by earlier lexicographers: *aroint thee* as a compression or corruption of *a raun to thee* – a verbal invocation of the power of rowan against witches.[36] As we shall see, it makes perfect sense that this should have been uttered by milkmaids – for milking and butter production, among the agricultural activities most vulnerable to magic attack, are also sites of intense folkloric belief in which the protective power of rowan is frequently deployed.

One man's witch, as James's typically patrician words on 'dafte wives' imply, is another's healer. Many prosecuted in Scotland were undoubtedly local service magicians who, whether as a result of disagreements or growing distrust of their methods, had been accused by neighbours or acquaintances of malevolence. Records from such trials give a tantalizing glimpse into the world of popular magic in early modern Britain, often including the counter-magical use of rowan. In 1607, Bartie Paterson admitted to having provided magical services to a range of clients. To one such customer, she gave nine 'pickles' (berries) of rowan, to carry on his person for protection.[37] Elizabeth Maxwell, tried in Dumfries in 1650, 'took a rowan over her head to cure a sickness', while, in the trial of Susan Hinchcliffe, heard at Woolley, Yorkshire, in 1674, an accuser testified to having overheard the accused lamenting a missed opportunity to harm one Thomas Bramhall – 'they tye soe much whighen [rowan] about him, I cannot come to my purpose'.[38]

The fascinating testimony of Isobell Watsonne, accused of witchcraft in 1590, includes a reference to having healed a case of worms with a charm made from rowan wood and – Shakespearean detail – a piece of finger taken from a corpse. Watsonne's evidence is also a notable example of how the witch's self-understanding was couched in a language quite different from that of her elite accusers. Her testimony speaks of meetings with the 'fair folk' (fairies), of change-lings and of a spirit consultant given the amusingly everyday name of Thomas Murray. According to the official theology of the judiciary, this could only be taken one way: as evidence of a satanic pact. For some contemporary scholars, however, the evidence of witches such as Isobell Watsonne implies the shadowy and longstanding existence of a visionary folk magic resembling shamanism. To read a witch's confession, they argue, is to experience complex folk beliefs being translated to fit the blunt interpretive framework – often imposed by torture – of judicial inquisitors. The visionary experience of tutelary spirits, for example, a widespread aspect of shamanic healing tradi-tions, becomes, under duress, a confession to cavorting with devils or the assumption of an animal familiar.[39] It has likewise been argued that witchcraft persecution was a way of combatting ingrained sources of female power, especially control over fertility.[40] Both approaches remind us of the difficulty and importance of unearthing sympathetic meanings beyond the persecutory view evinced in the legal record.

However we interpret witchcraft belief, it is a fact that the apo-tropaic use of rowan continued in Britain and Ireland well into the nineteenth century, being widely recorded by folklorists. Nowhere is this history more strikingly illustrated than by the various rowan amulets – including crosses and loops – donated to the Pitt Rivers Museum in Oxford by the Yorkshire clergyman, memoirist and anti-quarian J. C. Atkinson in 1893.[41] In a memoir of his incumbency at the remote moorland parish of Danby, an eccentric trove of vernac-ular lore and language, Atkinson noted that though 'witch-wood' was gathered almost exclusively from rowans, 'all was not "witch-wood" that was of the rowan': 'the "witch-wood", to be effectual . . . must be cut in due season . . . due place, and with due observances'.[42]

The efficacy of a rowan charm, in other words, was not solely dependent on a magical property of the wood, but relied also on the performance of magical actions and observance of correct procedure. To illustrate this, Atkinson records being told of an elderly woman of his parish, Hannah, being unexpectedly met in the 'wild solitudes' of the 'Head of the dale', a 'rugged and picturesque' location a good distance from her home. She was gathering 'witch-wood' for 'the upper sill of the house-door' and for 'the corresponding position as to stable, cow-byre, and the other domiciles of various stock'. She would also make, she reported, a charm 'for personal use . . . for the head of the bed, . . . the house place, etc.'.[43] For this witch-wood to be effective, she explained, it had to be taken from a tree the gatherer had never seen or been informed of; it was to be cut with a household knife and carried home by a route entirely distinct from the outward journey – and all this on St Helen's Day at the end of August, when the trees would likely, and significantly, have been in berry. Quite an investment of time, effort and, in such a remote place, risk.

Demand for magical protection, as Hannah's story clarifies, was focused both temporally and spatially: it was needed precisely at *thresholds* – thresholds in the spaces of farm and buildings, thresholds in the year. The health and safety of livestock was of utmost concern to rural people. For an agricultural labourer, supplementary income and food from animal products could mean the difference between starvation and survival; for pastoralists, especially in hill country or northern forests, there was constant anxiety about the loss of animals.

It is little wonder, then, that rowan rites and charms were so common at times of seasonal transition crucial in the welfare of

Rowan amulet donated to the Pitt Rivers Museum in Oxford by Canon J. C. Atkinson in 1893.

Beltane bonfire held at Calton Hill, Edinburgh. Rowan has diverse associations with this important seasonal festival.

sheep and cattle. Of particular importance here is the Celtic festival of Beltane, celebrated on the first day of May and, though most prominent in Scotland, Wales and Ireland, also known from Celtic regions of England – especially in Devon and Cornwall.[44] Traditionally, this was a time of bonfires, often kindled with rowan, lit to mark the seasonal departure of herds for upland summer pastures and to protect them against malefic spirits. As well as driving animals between the fires, the men would walk sun-wise round them, carrying branches of rowan. In his *Flora Scotica* of 1777, John Lightfoot records that, in the Highlands, the cattle would be driven to the shielings with a rowan rod, the rod itself then placed above the doors of the bothies where the herders lived and slept. In Strathspey, on the first day of May, he wrote, all the sheep and lambs would be passed through a hoop of rowan.[45] Similar rites are recorded in many northern regions, in Scandinavia and Germany especially, in which pastoralism was the predominant rural economy – places where seasonal transhumance was a central ritual of life.[46]

It was also at this time that milk might be churned into butter, an aspect of rural economy perhaps more marked with supernatural and magical associations than any other.[47] Some believed, for example, that at May Eve, a witch might steal the substance of a cow's milk, making it resistant to the butter churn; alternatively, a witch might assume the shape of a hare to take the milk – an idea widespread across Europe. A bewitched cow would yield blood in place of milk.[48] The Schools' Collection of the Irish Folklore Archive – some 740,000 pages of oral lore collected by primary school children in the Irish Free State between 1937 and 1939 – reveals the prevalence of precautions taken against such misfortune in rural Ireland, most of them focused around Beltane:

> On May Eve the farmer cuts rowan-berry in the shape of a ring and ties it to the cow's tail with a red string. It is an old belief that the butter would be taken of the milk if rowan-berry was not tied on the cow's tail.[49]

> In some neighbourhoods the people won't churn on May Day, except the churn is decorated with Rowan tree.[50]

> It was an old custom in this district to go round the fields on May morning and gather all the young rowan tree quicks. Out of each quick a ring was made. One of these rings along with a piece of red rag and a horse-shoe nail was tied to each cow's tail . . . Evil-minded people used to walk through the fields on May morning carrying a 'Sugan' or straw rope and by saying certain magic words they could take the milk from their neighbours' cows or the butter from the churn. It was necessary therefore to make use of the rowan trees and other things to prevent this.[51]

On the Isle of Man, the May Eve tradition of making a protective *crosh cuirn* (rowan cross) and placing it above the thresholds continues to the present day. As in many Celtic cultures, the rowan wood must be broken rather than cut from the tree.[52] In Scandinavia, according to the nineteenth-century anthropologist Sir James Frazer, wood from epiphytic or 'flying' rowans was believed especially effective in such charms, being 'placed over doors to prevent the ingress of witches'.[53]

It was not just witches that needed to be warded off. In Celtic regions especially, it was the fairies, the *sìth* or *sídhe* (pronounced *shee*), who were thought to steal the substance or benefit from the milk – a property known in Scottish Gaelic as its *toradh* – so that it would not satisfy or yielded no butter. Both animals and persons could be 'elf-taken', their real selves carried away by fairies and replaced with an empty simulacrum. A cow so struck, the Scottish folklorist John Gregorson Campbell reported, 'consume[d] the provender laid before it, but [did] not yield milk or grow fat'; 'it [gave] milk, but milk that yields no butter.'[54] A child, stolen by the fairies, was replaced with a tetchy and capricious changeling, its appetite never satisfied. Childbirth and nursing were especially risky moments, with either the mother or child liable to be taken. At such times, local women 'gathered and watched for three days' at least, and took 'various additional precautions', making rowan charms against the fairies.[55] After birth, many young mothers would have had no choice but to carry out domestic labour, often away from the home, leaving the infant to sleep. At such times, the child was especially exposed to fairy threat and needed the additional protection of 'rowan or coloured threads, or the sprinkling of *maistir*, urine, which was collected for use in waulking cloth'.[56] Throughout Scotland, rowans have long been planted near houses as a source of magical protection. Many would still hesitate to fell such a tree.[57]

In northern Finland, the otherworld threat was posed by forest spirits. This was especially the case, as in Scotland, when grazing animals were let out to new pastures: the beginning of summer, when cows would be released into the forest margin – a charged zone between the civilized and the wild – was an especially tense moment of magical negotiation.[58] A lost cow was believed to be hidden in the 'forest cover' – to have entered a parallel dimension in which spirits held their

Crosh cuirn from the Isle of Man. Ideally the rowan twigs are bound with wool gathered from hedgerows, fences and walls.

society. In Finnish folklore, the worlds of humans and forest spirits are parallel and analogous, with a fragile balance needing to be negotiated between them: charms and tales communicate an idea of the ecological give-and-take between the domesticated and wild, providing a model for reciprocity and equilibrium within the community.[59] If a human suffered some illness or misfortune, for example, this was not an arbitrary event, but was usually traceable to an offence given to the elemental powers, such as a curse uttered carelessly in frustration or pain. In such instances, magical negotiations, including tracing the moment and location of the triggering slight, would be carried out by the shaman (*tietäjä*), usually according to a model of mutual respect and diplomatic conciliation.

Finnish charms for the safety of grazing animals often temper their demands with ostentatious courtesy. This one, collected from a Karelian Christian named Marina Takalo, addresses the bear (or wolf) as spirit royalty to be calmed with a spoken muzzle of rowan:

Golden king of the forest

. . .

Don't attack my stock,
Don't touch my stock,
Wander over the wild tracks,
Canter across the animalless groves.
When you hear the sound of the bell,
Press your snout into the peat,
Quarry rocks with your claws,
Split rock with your claws,
Bite stones, tear tree trunks,
Hew cliffs!
But don't attack my stock!

. . .

I press a muzzle of rowan wood
Around the snub of your nose.[60]

Väinö Blomstedt, *Episode from the Kalevala: Kullervo Carving the Trunk of an Oak*, 1897, tempera on canvas. Blomstedt's painting shows cattle in traditional Finnish forest pasture, watched over by a lakeside rowan.

Sometimes, as with any diplomatic relation, good feeling could break down. It was always possible that the spirits would refuse to play by the rules and, in cases where conciliatory charms had failed, the *tietäjä* was entitled to rougher measures. One commonly used method was to 'bind' the forest, a way of forcing it to reveal the source of an illness or to return a lost animal: ropes would be tied in symbolic fashion to trees or rocks and an accusatory spell spoken. In one version of such a charm, 'two rowan trees opposite each other' are used to represent 'the forest master's testicles'.[61] Here, surely, is an example of the good humour, a spirit of irony and play, which often infuses folklore: laughter is an especially effective remedy against any misfortune not likely to be overly disastrous. It should give us pause to remember that often an informer may have wished to pull the scholarly folklorist's leg. Credulity is not exclusively a property of 'traditional' belief, and a great deal of folklore comes with a measure of inbuilt scepticism and knowing irony. Rather than offering an unfailing or prescriptive guide to effective action, folklore serves both as a vivid reminder of just how much is beyond human control and as a focus for solidarity against the intrusions of dominant or elite culture.[62]

Indeed, we must now ask what logics and motivations bind the many ritual and magic acts just discussed and consider the particular significance of rowan in these practices. Generalization is no doubt risky. The meaning of any act, even identically performed, is likely to be somewhat specific to the individual carrying it out, while the same charm made in different historical times might have entirely distinct psychological resonances: it might be motivated by genuine fear or belief; it might provide a focus for the communication and negotiation of ideas and norms; it might confer distinction on the possessor of specialized knowledge or promote allegiance to a particular tradition; it may be simple habit. Some broad theories, nevertheless, can be proposed.

One argument about witchcraft accusations in early modern Britain is that they resulted from a weakening of traditional forms of social solidarity, such as the giving of alms. Widespread agricultural enclosures, leading to poverty and unemployment, placed many at the mercy of their neighbours, just as individualism and a Protestant morality of work weakened the imperative to give.[63] Elderly women were often victims of cruel poverty, especially if widowed. Where they petitioned alms and were denied, many may have uttered curses or insults in anger and desperation. If the memory of a strong obligation to charity could still raise a spectre of moral shame, genuine psychosomatic symptoms could result – so that the curse would seem effective in itself. The making of a rowan charm – especially where the sourcing of the material involved complex ritual prescriptions, the sacrifice of effort and time – might act to discharge ambivalent social emotions. The ritual act helps soothe the guilt and anxiety accompanying personal good fortune, the knowledge that others suffer. More broadly, any ritual performance can serve to mitigate anxiety in situations where no more certain method exists to ward off the unpredictable, brutally common tragedy.

Ritual complexity likely also has a mnemonic function, serving to promote fastidiousness and care in the performance of the most important household tasks. A housewife, asked why she is tying rowan to her butter churn, has occasion to tell a story about the moment's significance and the uncertainties surrounding it – recourse to witches and fairies being more conducive to memory and attention than a transactional or materialist account.

With their accompanying story and lore, charms are also a focus for the communication of morals and norms, often repressive: they serve as emblematic reminders of a disciplinary function that permeates the social but starts at home. It is scarcely surprising that the dairy was a focus for superstition and recrimination – it was one of the few areas of life in rural societies in which women held a measure of extra-domestic power. Selling butter and milk and negotiating their prices, women played a role, prior to the market-mechanism, in establishing terms of fair exchange and earning their own income. In small communities, such situations brought repressive ideas about gender into dangerous proximity with valued principles of neighbourly equity. Where a woman seemed excessively forceful or ambitious in such endeavours, where her pursuit of personal interest, perhaps through haggling or barter, was deemed improper – even unfeminine – she might well find herself accused of witchcraft; one study has found that around 80 per cent of Scottish accusations were tied in some way to this sphere of women's work.[64] A similar idea is expressed in the medieval motif of the 'devil's milkmaid', found in Scandinavian church murals, which depicted those who had unusual success in dairy production as being assisted by devils. Witch beliefs, therefore, could carry a disciplinary function, tying repressive ideals of feminine behaviour to the navigation of neighbourly resentments and inequalities of fortune. What is a witch, after all, but one who has betrayed the sanctity of marriage for the erotic temptations of Satan – a shortcut to personal empowerment? Perhaps this is why rowan, symbolic of idealized femininity, is so often enlisted as a defence against the transgression of gender embodied by the malevolent witch.

Fairy beliefs are also a focus for this negotiation of norms. The discourse of the *toradh* or substance of household goods, central to fairy lore in the Highlands and Islands, was not concerned with the nature of the object alone: the essence of milk or simple bread is lost when a person becomes dissatisfied with their lot – where they take no benefit or pleasure in what God has provided.[65] The fairy society of such popular lore is a mirror of quasi-aristocratic luxury as prevalently imagined by critics of urban decadence and vice: the *sìth* live a hedonism without substance, in which everything is glitter and show. To be 'away with the fairies' was to be carried off by unsubstantial dreams, to want what you could not have. Behind this code is a spartan claim about the value of hardship and perseverance, a form of rugged pride. It speaks of solidarity too – for most peasant societies were bound by notions of a rough egalitarianism, with folklore acting as a mechanism for mitigating envy, encouraging ideas of reciprocity and equalizing resources: any advancement, any desire to

Woman churns butter assisted by devils. Gothic fresco in Västra Vemmerlöv church, Sweden. Few areas of domestic labour made more use of rowan charms.

have more than one's neighbours, was considered sin – hence, in the Finnish examples, the overall ethic of balance in dealing with the spirits.[66] There is a double logic to the rowan's association with fairies in this case. The berries, being showy but essentially inedible to humans, are, for this very reason, archetypal fairy food. But the beauty of a local rowan, too, is an emblem of what glories the local can provide – a gift given freely and for all. Gathered and brought home, the piece of rowan, with its berries or blossom, offers a reminder of this kind of gratitude, a psychic defence against 'the fairy'.

Behind these scattered references to rowan's magical and apotropaic uses lies an obscure region of suffering and loss. Much of the folk narrative in which rowan is involved is charged with the terror of arbitrary rupture in the fabric of life. Tales of mothers taken by fairies during birth or pregnancy, of changeling children lost or left in the wild – all are skewed transmissions from the obscure history of existence under the pressure of endemic famine and disease; they deal with post-natal depression, with psychosis and hysteria, with unexplainable illness and congenital deformity, with the simple inability to carry on as normal. Folklore offered a way to talk about what was difficult or taboo – what was almost too much to bear. For many who turned to it for comfort and protection, the rowan must have been a last resort, an emblem of weakest hope.

three
Arts of Nationhood
🪡

I n the late 1930s, Mary Hegarty, a schoolgirl from Donegal, was
asked to transcribe her homework onto the fresh pages of a large
memorandum book. That week, Mary had made a note of riddles and games known in her home village, Burnfoot. Though much
of the material came from relatives and friends, a short entry on
'Homemade Toys' seems to record Mary's own personal reflections.[1]
'There are not many ways that I know of for boys and girls to make
toys at home,' she writes, but 'a way of making a necklace is to gather
Rowan berries . . . and put a needle through the centre of the berries
and then put a thread through each one in turn'.[2]

Mary's evocative words are preserved in one of over 1,000 handwritten volumes, compiled between 1937 and 1939, which today form
the Schools' Collection of the Irish Folklore Archives. Part of a broad
heritage initiative legislated by the newly independent republic, the
scheme was the brainchild of two men, Séamus Ó Duilearga and
Seán Ó Súilleabháin, director and registrar, respectively, of the Irish
Folklore Commission. The governing assumptions of the project are
ably condensed in the foreword to the booklet of instructions sent
to participating institutions:

> The collection of the oral traditions of the Irish people is a
> work of national importance . . . rescuing from oblivion the
> traditions which, in spite of the vicissitudes of the historic
> Irish nation, have, century in, century out, been preserved

Illustration by J. S. Eland, from Hilda Murray, *Flower Legends for Children* (1901).

with loving care by their ancestors. The task is an urgent one for in our time most of this important national oral heritage will have passed away for ever.[3]

Today, it may seem uncontroversial that a government should play some sponsoring role in preserving national culture. But it is easy to underestimate the historical peculiarity of such an archival impulse. Before the eighteenth century, it would have been almost unthinkable to suggest that a child's game could be considered a matter 'of national importance'.

So what had changed? The short answer is that, between the eighteenth and twentieth centuries, a new vision of the nation had taken shape: a vision in which an elusive patriotic spirit was imagined to animate the lives and customs of ordinary people, their mores and folkways preserving an archaic religiosity with potentially regenerative powers in an age of aggressive materialism.[4] In this chapter, we consider the place of the rowan tree in the formation, articulation and negotiation of such a discourse – in the matter of cultural nationalisms across northern Europe, and specifically in Scotland, Ireland and Finland.

As a historical ideal, this vision of nationality marched in step with the political emergence of the modern nation-state. For many historians of nationalism, the trend towards national self-determination is best explained as part of a broader narrative of modernization: the nation-state is a logical corollary of constitutionalism, representative government and the rise of a commercial society; it is made possible by advances in communications and infrastructure, media and literacy.[5] All this is true, but it is only half the story. Throughout this chapter, we explore an antiquarian and folkloric impulse that has continually shadowed, and often fed into, the modernizing ideals of political nationhood, making it possible for artists and writers to find new symbolic meanings for the rowan.

Mary Hegarty's handwritten account of 'Homemade Toys'.

Carolina Oliphant, Lady Nairne, illustration from Charles Rogers, ed., *Life and Songs of the Baroness Nairne* (1896).

In the early nineteenth century, one signal manifestation of emergent nationalisms was the rising popularity of anthologies of 'national' poetry and song. Written by the Scottish songwriter Carolina Oliphant, Lady Nairne, 'The Rowan Tree' first appeared pseudonymously in 1822 as part of one such collection, *The Scotish Minstrel*. Depicting a world that Mary Hegarty would have recognized – including a rowan necklace – the song has gained a lasting place in Scottish national consciousness:

> O ROWAN tree, O rowan tree! thou'lt aye be dear to
> me!
> Intwined thou art wi' mony ties o' hame and infancy.
> Thy leaves were aye the first o' spring, thy flowers
> the simmer's pride;
> There wasna sic a bonnie tree in a' the country side.
> O rowan tree!

How fair wert thou in simmer time, wi' a' thy
    clusters white,
How rich and gay thy autumn dress, wi' berries red
    and bright!
On thy fair stem were mony names which now nae
    mair I see,
But they're engraven on my heart—forgot they ne'er
    can be!
    O rowan tree!

We sat aneath thy spreading shade, the bairnies
    round thee ran,
They pu'd thy bonnie berries red, and necklaces they
    strang.
My mother! O I see her still, she smiled our sports
    to see,
Wi' little Jeanie on her lap, and Jamie at her knee.
    O rowan tree!

O there arose my father's prayer, in holy evening's
    calm;
How sweet was then my mother's voice in the
    Martyr's psalm!
Now a' are gane! we meet na mair aneath the rowan
    tree!
But hallowed thoughts around thee twine o' hame
    and infancy.
    O rowan tree![6]

On the surface, this is a deeply personal lyric. Its nostalgic depiction of Nairne's childhood at Gask House, Perthshire, simmers with
pathos: seasons pass, day turns to 'holy' evening, and 'mony names'
melt into oblivion, but the rowan stands as a talisman, granting access
to 'hallowed' memories. As we will see, however, 'The Rowan Tree'

also has a political significance, knowingly participating in 'national' discourse. Appropriating the tree's wider cultural significations – its close association with domestic protection, with 'ties o' hame and infancy' – Nairne makes the rowan a focus for critical ideas about nationhood, contesting the vision of Scotland implicit in the country's assimilation to an Anglo-centric *British* nationhood.

First of all, there is the song's subtle self-referentiality. Through the use of the refrain 'o rowan tree', Nairne has us repeatedly invoke the song's title; the apostrophized rowan subtly merges with the lyric itself. It is a formal move, which implies a parallel between the personal solace offered by the tree and the cultural work of song, a notion also cleverly referenced in the second verse. By referring to words first inscribed on the rowan and then 'engraved' in the 'heart' of the speaker, Nairn gestures to the alternation of writing and oral performance in the preservation of song traditions. Even where written versions are lost, songs can be preserved by loving memory – by 'heart' – and repeated performance: the rowan becomes a symbol of this survival of communal consciousness.

Transcending its formulaic subject-matter, 'The Rowan Tree' says something subtle and interesting about the life and origins of shared meaning. Offering a personal record of the reciprocal emotions and significations that flow between people and the ecology they inhabit, it imagines this interchange as a microcosm of communal solidarity: the rowan *gives* something to the family – beauty, joy, the berries for a necklace, a place to gather in prayer – which brings them closer to one another. Finally, by the resources of art, something is invested back into the tree, changing the way it can be known and lending emotional potency to future encounters with rowan for those who share such traditions.

Promoting an idealized community, 'The Rowan Tree' was also participating in a projective fabrication: the song was Nairne's original creation, not an immemorial artefact of rural life. Readers of collections such as *Scotish Minstrel* were, in fact, often willing participants in a widespread literary deception, reading new songs as relics of ancient

Engraving based on a sketch of the 'auld house' at Gask by Lady Nairne, from Charles
Rogers, ed., *Life and Songs of the Baroness Nairne* (1896). The rowan tree is just visible
on the left, sheltering the lonely wayfarer.

orality. Though the volume's preface proclaims the authentically
Scottish heritage of its songs, many were written by the editor, R. A.
Smith.[7] Yet the very act of fabrication speaks to the complex cultural
politics of the era. Just as, in 'The Rowan Tree', Nairne transmutes
personal memory into something with wider communal resonances,
the majority of artists and writers in the emergent 'national' tradition
seem to have believed in the possibility that their work, though new,
could revive an authentic ancestral spirit.

It was an idea that received its most influential formulations just
over half a century earlier, as proto-Romantic figures, including the
Scottish poet James Macpherson and the German philologist and
theologian Johann Gottfried von Herder, began to challenge prevailing Enlightenment notions of history. While thinkers such as Adam
Smith proposed that the social sentiments needed for successful
nationhood could only be created by the development of a mercantile
society, both Macpherson and Herder presented commercialism as
a regression from ancestral solidarities. In the 1760s, Macpherson

Oh! rowan tree, oh! rowan tree.

THE ROWAN TREE.*

Verses by Lady NAIRNE.

1. Oh! row-an tree, oh! ro-wan tree, thou'lt aye be dear to me, En-twin'd thou art wi' mo-ny ties, O!
2. How fair wert thou in simmer-time, wi' a' thy clusters white; How rich and gay thy autumn dress, wi'
3. We sat aneath thy spreading shade, the bairnies round thee ran, They pu'd thy bon-nie berries red, and
4. Oh! there a-rose my father's pray'r, in ho-ly evening's calm, How sweet was then my mither's voice,

1. hame and in - fan-cy. Thy leaves were aye the first o' spring, thy flow'rs the simmer's pride; There
2. ber - ries red and bright. On thy fair stem were mo - ny names, which now nae mair I see, But
3. neck-la - ces they strang. My mi - ther, O! I see her still, she smil'd our sports to see, Wi'
4. in the mar-tyr's psalm. Now a' are gane! we meet nae mair, a - neath the row-an tree; But

1. was nae sic a bon-nie tree in a' the coun-try side; Oh! row - an tree!
2. they're en-gra - ven on my heart,—for-got they ne'er can be! Oh! row - an tree!
3. lit - tle Jea - nie on her lap, wi' Ja - mie at her knee! Oh! row - an tree!
4. hal-low'd thoughts around thee twine o' hame and in - fan-cy, Oh! row - an tree!

* Lady Carolina Nairne was born at the house of Gask, Perthshire, in 1766. She was the daughter of Lawrence Oliphant, of Gask, a staunch Jacobite, who had followed Prince Charlie through the '45, and always spoke of King George as the Elector of Hanover. In 1806 she married Captain N. W. Nairne, a second cousin, and a son of one of the young Chevalier's adherents. He became Lord Nairne in 1824, and died in 1830. Lady Nairne survived him till 1845, when she died in her seventy-ninth year. No one was more shy of a literary reputation than Lady Nairne. Her best songs were contributed to R. A. Smith's *Scottish Minstrel*, 1822, under the *nom de plume* of B. B.—" Mrs. Bogan of Bogan," and so close did she guard her secret, that not even the Editor of that work was aware of the name and position of his contributor. For years her songs were introduced into collections of Scottish songs without any mention of the author's name. This, however, is now changed, and Lady Nairne has taken her place as a song writer beside Burns, Hogg, and Tannahill.

Words and music to 'The Rowan Tree', as presented in Alfred Moffat, ed., *The Minstrelsy of Scotland* (1895).

delighted and outraged his contemporaries by presenting a series of 'ancient' Gaelic epics in cadent English prose (they were, in fact, creative re-renderings of Gaelic manuscript material). Imbuing the archaic Celtic heroes with fine feelings and a gentle, melancholic sentimentality, these seemed to suggest that history was not so progressive as Smith imagined.

A literary sensation on the continent, Macpherson's writings stimulated a ferment of proto-nationalist theorizing and, in the figure of Ossian, helped create an archetypal image of the ancient Celtic bard. But it was Herder who most eloquently condensed the cultural-nationalist idea of folk song. 'All nations', he wrote, 'that have yet to be organised around political systems are a singing people . . . Songs serve as collections for all their *science, religion,* the ways the soul *moves* . . . the *joys* and *sorrows* of their lives.' The revival of folk song, he believed, would restore a vision of the 'people in its naked simplicity, the happiness with which it was born'; it would unveil 'nature in its most basic creative potential', clearing away the 'artificiality . . . and false politeness that . . . generate an inhumane sense of bourgeois life'.[8] With Herder, song becomes a viable engine of national revival.

By Nairne's time, Herder's influence had diffused itself into the atmosphere of nationalist discourse, giving licence to the idea of new literary creations claiming common origin with an archaic national spirit – of re-awakening some 'basic creative potential'. A prevailing sense of tradition as that which is always about 'to have passed away for ever' – as Ó Súilleabháin's preface puts it – made creative licence a matter of urgency: just as Macpherson's Ossian was the last hero of his culture, singing of a vanished age, so 'The Rowan Tree' assumes a perspective of mournful survival. The sense of belatedness had particular piquancy in Scotland. Here was a land with its own proud history as an independent *kingdom* negotiating its emergence as a fully modern nation as part of a Union, legislated in 1707, that many saw as shamefully subordinating.[9] As many Scots prospered in the machinery of British state and empire, the revival of specifically 'Scottish' song was evidence of growing confidence and pride in

Broadside cartoon from the aftermath of Culloden. Britannia, in the middle, decides between mercy and butchery. Bonnie Prince Charlie stands on the left, surrounded by Jacobite emblems.

national culture; but it also revealed insecurities stemming from a union in which Scotland was often portrayed in the position of an unwilling bride.[10]

For Lady Nairne, and many Scots, there was an additional element to such ambivalence: Jacobitism. When, in 1688, English parliamentarians invited William of Orange to take the throne of England – to ensure that James II's Catholic son, James Edward Stuart, would not inherit it – they enshrined a commitment to two things as essential to British politics: parliamentary monarchy and a Protestant ruler. In 1707 and 1714, such principles were strongly reaffirmed, first by the Act of Union and then by the installation of George I, Elector of Hanover, to succeed the childless Queen Anne.[11]

Lady Nairne's family, however, were loyal to the exiled House of Stuart and the political-theological principle of absolutist heredity. In this, they found common cause with many of the Highland clans, whom they joined in successive unsuccessful rebellions in support of the Stuart claimants in 1715 and 1745.[12] Defeat by the Duke of Cumberland at Culloden in 1745 put an end to armed Jacobitism as a military threat, initiating a brutal state-sponsored backlash.

top: In Scotland, rowans have traditionally been planted on the north side of houses to provide magical protection for the inhabitants. Today, such trees often serve as a melancholy reminder of forgotten lives and communities.

bottom: Ruined croft at Moss of Tolophin, Aberdeenshire, Scotland.

Through military occupation, confiscation of lands, and financial measures designed to ensure that land-holding in the Highlands would operate on commercial principles, Jacobite defeat accelerated the termination of clanship as an economic and social reality in Scotland.[13] After the '45, Nairne's father and grandfather were forced into a seventeen-year exile in France before they returned, significantly impoverished, to their Perthshire home at Gask.

Nairne's childhood at Gask, memorialized in 'The Rowan Tree', was indelibly marked by her family's Stuart loyalism. Once we are aware of this background, it becomes clear that sympathetic identification with Jacobitism is a powerful subtext in the song.[14] The mention of 'many names' written on the rowan surely refers to the loyalists killed in defence of their true king, as does the mention of a 'Martyr's psalm' sung by the gathered family. The rowan's colours – white and red – are those of Stuart loyalty and martyrdom. By describing the tree as 'bonnie', Nairne references a familiar invocation of the Young Pretender.

Nairne's rowan is thus a powerfully dynastic emblem, a coded reference to the hereditary monarch as a source of legitimate social cohesion and protector of his people. In Jacobite iconography, the Stuarts were frequently associated with the oak, a symbol derived from the Boscobel Oak which, according to royalist lore, had sheltered Charles II. Nairne, however, both Scotticizes the symbol and gives it a feminine twist. Focusing her negotiation of nationhood on the domestic and familial, she affirms a principle uniting the divine right monarchy with the clan society so loyal to the Stuarts: the sense of nationhood as an extension of clanship, its commonality derived from (mythical) shared ancestry and from ties of affection reinforced, in spite of hierarchy, by participation in rites of kinship.[15]

It is easy to dismiss the products of cultural nationalism as sentimental and reactionary.[16] However, there are aspects of this idea of culture that articulate important dissonances at the heart of commercial society.[17] Many of Nairne's lyrics develop a stern criticism of nascent capitalism by chastising an urban elite who, in her satirical depictions, pursue enrichment at the expense of poorer Scots and in betrayal of local solidarities.[18] Perhaps her most affecting song is 'Caller Herrin'', a lyric that gives voice to a working fishwife as she tries desperately to sell the herring brought in by brave Scottish fishermen, now scorned by 'ladies, clad in silk and laces'. The fishermen, Nairne so incisively realizes, are exposed to more than the sea: the real storm they have to weather is market forces, which would increasingly govern the lives of an emerging working class.

Over the next century, such pressures only intensified. As clan society collapsed, landlords were effectively forced to pursue profit at the expense of old loyalties, ejecting tenants and cottars from their lands to make way for sheep. Many Scots moved to the cities, others chose to emigrate to Canada and the USA. 'The Rowan Tree' has survived the test of time because it tapped into a sense of displacement, which would become more and more common in Scottish experience. Today, many rowans still stand as melancholy monuments of clearance. Dotted around abandoned townships, the last markers of former gardens, they are a record of care and affection for the home place.

Seventy years after the publication of Nairne's song, William Butler Yeats, then 27, wrote a letter to a friend describing a 'magical adventure' on a beach near Sligo. Accompanied by his uncle, George Pollexfen, and a cousin, Lucy Middleton, he had seen a host of fairies carrying rowan berries:

> a cave by the Rosses sands . . . I made a magical circle & invoked the fairys . . . a great sound as of little people cheering & stamping with their feet away in the heart of the rock. The queen of the troop came then . . . & held a long conversation with us & finally wrote in the sand 'be careful & do not seek to know too much about us' . . . One troop of the creatures carried quicken berries in their hands.[19]

Like Nairne's, Yeats's work gathers meaning from the context of national politics. This passage is no exception, revealing characteristic aspects of Yeats's idea of Ireland. At the time, the young poet was collecting local folklore, which would later become *The Celtic Twilight*, first published in 1893. His approach was motivated by the belief that magical activity and the propagation of occult knowledge could unearth a specifically Irish form of spiritual revelation – a revelation that he earnestly believed would be of value to the nationalist cause.[20]

Clearly, however, there was also some subconscious sense of danger or ambivalence in Yeats's pursuit of these aims. Not long after the fairy queen's warning to him on the beach at Rosses Point, he penned some verses in which rowan berries, again, appear as a natural entity straddling the material–spiritual divide. Here, however, they represent a dangerous temptation:

> Beloved, hear my bitter tale! –
> Now making busy with the oar,
> Now flinging loose the slanting sail,
> I hurried from the woody shore,
> And plucked small fruits on Innisfree.
> (Ah, mournful Danaan quicken tree!)
>
> A murmuring faery multitude,
> When flying to the heart of light
> From playing hurley in the wood
> With creatures of our heavy night,
> A berry threw for me – or thee.
> (Ah, mournful Danaan quicken tree!)
>
> And thereon grew a tender root,
> And thereon grew a tender stem,
> And thereon grew the ruddy fruit
> That are a poison to all men

And meat to the Aslauga Shee.
(Ah, mournful Danaan quicken tree!)

If when the battle is half won,
I fling away my sword, blood dim,
Or leave some service all undone,
Beloved blame the Danaan whim,
And blame the snare they set for me.
(Ah, mournful Danaan quicken tree!)

Cast out all hope, cast out all fear,
And taste with me the faeries' meat,
For while I blamed them I could hear
Dark Joan call the berries sweet,
Where Niam heads the revelry.
(Ah, mournful Danaan quicken tree!)[21]

Composed in March or April 1893, 'The Danaan Quicken Tree' was published in *The Bookman* in May the same year. Yeats never included the poem in his printed volumes, so it is clear he thought it of limited value as a lasting record of his art. It is, however, of considerable interest as a revelation of the author's own state of mind – and as a marker of the increasing prominence of the rowan in the legendary flora of Romantic Celticism in the late nineteenth century.

In 1893, Yeats was approaching thirty. He had achieved a measure of recognition in Ireland for poems, plays and a novel, *John Sherman*, all of which drew heavily on folklore and early Irish literature – 'Celtic romance', he called it. These youthful works present the fairy otherworld as a refuge from the utilitarianism of contemporary culture, offering a utopian vision of ancestral nationhood. Yeats's artistic thinking was a development of cultural-nationalist tenets prominent since the 1830s, especially those associated with the Young Ireland movement, which the poet joined in the 1880s.[22] Founded by a group of mixed Protestant and Catholic journalists and lawyers in 1842,

Ireland's west coast as landscape of enchantment: *Children Dancing on the Strand*, 1914, oil on canvas, by Yeats's friend and collaborator George William Russell (Æ).

Young Ireland aimed to supplement political agitation – for repeal of the 1800 Acts of Unions – with a social activism capable of inspiring cultural revival. Arguing that centuries of English exploitation had tragically divided and weakened authentic Irish life, the movement articulated a forceful vision for the establishment of a decentralized, rural and self-sufficient nation.[23]

By the 1890s, buoyed by a great acceleration of scholarly and philological interest in early Irish texts, Yeats had begun to flesh out his own occultist version of such an agenda. Committed to separatist neo-Fenian politics, and inspired by an obsessive love for the beautiful and charismatic radical Maud Gonne, the young poet had visions of literature as a central engine of national politics. He himself, of course, would preside over such efforts. In 1891, Yeats made the practical step of helping found an Irish Literary Society in London. The following year, he hurried to Dublin, hoping to involve himself in the establishment of a sister branch of the society, consolidating his literary and political programme. The attempt, however, backfired. Lampooned in the conservative press, and ousted from any piloting role in the National Literary Society, Yeats found himself at bay. His relationship with Gonne provided little consolation; she had never shown much interest in loving him back, and in the first few months of 1893, they suffered a falling out that would lead to an extended period of mutual alienation.[24] It was a time Yeats later remembered as 'one of great trouble'.[25]

Such circumstances help explain the strange reversal in Yeats's use of fairy material in 'The Danaan Quicken Tree'. Fairyland, long Yeats's emblem of an idealized Ireland, is transformed into a poisonous temptation: the poem draws on the folklore of rowan as a fairy tree to present a sense of despair over the very attempt to repurpose legendary material for cultural regeneration – 'I fling away my sword.' It is the petulant announcement of the poet's desire to quit the business of national literary politics.

From the perspective of Yeats's later career, the wobble of 'The Danaan Quicken Tree' would seem a minor episode in a lasting commitment to Irish revivalism. He must have quickly found it embarrassingly self-pitying, especially its histrionic address to Maud Gonne – 'Beloved, hear my bitter tale!' It is hardly surprising that he expunged it from the canon of his collected verse. But aside from the insight it provides into Yeats's journey, what is historically significant about 'The Danaan Quicken Tree' is that, even though it presents Yeats's relation to folklore and myth negatively, it is the rowan that the poem unequivocally proposes as the tradition's representative tree.

As we've seen, the rowan features in many early Irish texts. It clearly had longstanding associations with magic. However, Yeats and his collaborators projected the rowan's contemporary folkloric prominence back into the mists of pagan deep time, reimagining the tree as practically *the* magical and mythic species in Irish tradition. It is a reimagining that remains influential today, informing both contemporary neo-pagan engagements with rowan and the familiar iconography of gift-shop Celticism.

Despite his fay aura, Yeats's great strengths were perseverance and self-belief. By century's end, he had redoubled the hermetic intensity of his literary and political efforts, committing, with his friend, the writer, painter and mystic George Russell, to the creation of a New Age religious movement – the Order of Celtic Mysteries. Combining their antiquarian investigations into Irish 'myth' with material revealed by trance experiences, Yeats, Russell and others set out to create – or revive – ancient Druidical rites; they imagined their nascent Order as a spiritual aristocracy capable of seeding national renewal. Russell, in particular, was fired by the millenarian pronouncements of the contemporary Theosophist movement.[26]

In seeking to unearth these ancient rites, Yeats and Russell concocted a method that was in some sense a practical extension of widespread nineteenth-century assumptions about Irish 'myth' and folklore. They saw the legendary figures and heroes of the medieval stories, especially the semi-divine *Túatha dé*, as remnants of an ancient pantheon, interpreting the later fairies of folklore as echoes of the same beings. They therefore took the early texts as essentially outgrowths of archaic ritual culture, susceptible to inspired poetic exegesis.

One mythic figure, Aengus, attained special importance for the Order. Associated with youth, beauty and native poetry, he was also frequently linked to the rowan. In December 1898, Yeats recorded a vision of Aengus as a 'medieval fool . . . in a cap of pale violet . . . & pointed shoes. He held a long staff of the mountain ash . . . surmounted by a kind of caduceus shape.'[27] In Aengus's hands, the rowan is restored to full magico-mythic potency – an emblem of the power of imagination as a means of access to otherworldly wisdom.

As the century drew to a close, Russell, in particular, was responsible for a tremendous flood of articles and arcana, most published in the *Irish Theosophist* under his pseudonym, Æ. One such article, 'The Fountains of Youth', published in September 1897, places the rowan at the centre of a set of reflections typical of Russell's sense of national revival. The argument begins, characteristically, with a snippet of folklore: 'I heard', Russell reports, 'that a strange woman, dwelling on the western coast, who had the repute of healing by faery power, said a little before she died, "There's a cure for all things in the well at Ballykeele."[28] Taking the idea of a 'cure for all things' as its starting point, 'The Fountains of Youth' follows a chain of associations that connects natural beauty, mystical experience and ancient religion to the cultural work of the artist.

Sacred wells are common in Ireland, many shaded by 'clootie trees', often rowans, to which pilgrims attach shreds of cloth signifying prayers for saintly intercedence.[29] It is likely that many of these wells were also thought sacred before the arrival of Christianity.[30] Russell, however, proposes a naturalistic interpretation of the woman's statement: 'perhaps she had bent over the pool until its darkness grew wan and bright and troubled with the movements of a world within

Clootie tree in the Holy Well at Fore Abbey, County Westmeath, Ireland.

and the agitations of a tempestuous joy.' Looking into the pool is a 'cure' in that it offers the solace of beauty, transmuting life's 'agitations' into 'joy'. But Russell goes further: 'touched from within by the living beauty, the soul, the ancient Druid in man, renews its league with the elements.' If the higher soul is one with nature, he argues, then it was the wisdom of the Druids to harness this primal connection as a basis for social cohesion. The Irish artist's task, as Russell saw it, was a Druid-like conversion of aesthesis – the experience of natural beauty – into ritual, forging the ancient nation anew.

In 'The Fountains of Youth', rowan is made symbolically central to such an ambition. In the conclusion to the article, Russell suggests a connection between the woman's vision in the well at Ballykeele and the mythological 'Well of Connla'. In the early Irish material, this well, located in the spiritual otherworld, is the source of all the rivers of Ireland and an emblem of idealized continuity between worlds. The well is overgrown by nine sacred 'hazels of wisdom'. When these hazels shed their nuts into the water, they are eaten by migratory salmon. Swimming into the worldly realm, the boundary-crossing fish become a source of otherworldly wisdom for humans.[31]

In Russell's handling, the old woman's vision at Ballykeele becomes a powerful intuition of the archetypal significance of this legend. It reveals an essential connection between the possibility of communal renewal and a shared appreciation of natural aesthetics:

Perhaps the strange woman who spoke of the well at Ballykeele, and the others like her, may know more . . . than the legend-seekers who so learnedly annotated their tales . . . I think if that strange woman could have found a voice for what was in her heart she would have completed her vague oracle somewhat as I have done:

There's a cure for all things in the well at Ballykeele,
Where the scarlet cressets o'erhang from the rowan trees;

There's a joy-breath blowing from the Land of
    Youth I feel,
  And earth with its heart at ease.

Many and many a sun-bright maiden saw the
    enchanted land
With star-faces glimmer up from the druid wave:
Many and many a pain of love was soothed by a faery
    hand
  Or lost in the love it gave.

When the quiet with a ring of pearl shall wed the earth
And the scarlet berries burn dark by the stars in the
    pool,
Oh, its lost and deep I'll be in the joy-breath and the
    mirth,
  My heart in the star-heart cool.

Aptly condensing Russell's outlook on the task of the revivalist artist, 'The Fountains of Youth' substitutes the otherworld hazels of the Connla myth for more palpable rowans. Transforming the rowan's beauty into a source of imagined community, a 'cure for all things', it is a substitution richly indicative of the new centrality given to the tree in the occult-nationalist reimagining of Celtic mysteries.

From its Yeatsian wellspring, rowan imagery rippled outwards, not just into Irish writing and art, but also into a new wave of Celtic revivalism in Scotland – a current most prodigiously represented by the works of Fiona MacLeod, an alias of the Paisley-born writer William Sharp. It is no surprise to find, in the Scottish artist John Duncan's painting *The Riders of the Sídhe* (1911), that the foremost rider, likely Aengus himself, should be holding a luminous branch of rowan – an emblem of healing wisdom.

Duncan was doubtless influenced by Russell, and the parallels in their work are instructive. For all their heady aestheticism, both

John Duncan, *The Riders of the Sidhe*, 1911, tempera on canvas.

Duncan's painting and Russell's deep-image verses suffer from a sense of airlessness and arrest. Though apparently in motion, no rushing breezes stir the lavish drapery or luminous coiffure of Duncan's Gaelic gods; curiously without dynamism, each figure faces in a different solitary direction, their horses' hooves barely disturbing the earth. In Russell's poem, likewise, the moment of illumination is predicated on a stillness at odds with the yearned-for winds of change, the renovating 'joy-breath blowing from the Land of Youth'. Unlike the hazelnuts that drop into the Well of Connla, Russell's rowan berries are isolated from any dynamic ecology; frozen in an image, they are somehow as distant as stars.

As well as being a feature of technique, this lack of movement takes us to the heart of a disagreement between Russell and Yeats, which would become increasingly apparent as they worked on the Celtic Mysteries. For while Russell was predisposed to value moments of personal insight or enlightenment, content to luxuriate in the still image, Yeats was continually pushing to translate such visions into an active national force. Their different uses of the rowan as a symbol take us to the heart of this divergence. Though it is a potent emblem of the enchantment present in Irish nature, for Yeats, the rowan always stands as an ambivalent symbol: it is a cipher for the painful difficulty of mediating between personal enthusiasms – the *feeling* of spiritual insight – and the trickier negotiations of a worldly politics. Perhaps there was a good ecological reason for this. For the berries of rowan, though beautiful in the bare landscape of winter, are a conspicuous relic of more dynamic seasons of growth. To be taken with their fascination is to mistake an afterimage for the real principle of life.

In the mid-nineteenth century, cultural historians such as Ernest Renan and Matthew Arnold celebrated Celtic literature for its spiritual intensity and closeness to nature.[32] Yet they also presented it as evidence of a people that were both impractical and effeminate –

unfit, somehow, for the modern world. Yeats made it his mission to challenge this narrative, making the case for the pre-eminent contemporary importance of Celtic culture. He urged his readers to see the folkloric poetry of Ireland as surviving evidence of a single 'ancient world religion', its relict centres spread across the 'under-developed' regions of Europe. 'The Slavonic, the Finnish, the Scandinavian, and the Celtic' literatures, Yeats writes, striking a Herderian note, are 'fountains of the passions and beliefs of ancient times'.[33] Their combined wisdom, revived by nationalist art movements, would help inspire a higher civilizational synthesis of spiritual and materialist culture.

Although he was a nationalist, Yeats understood himself as part of a pan-European movement for cultural renewal, a movement compounded of syncretistic spirituality, symbolist rhetoric and heroic primitivism. In describing this cross-continental revival, Yeats sets up the Finnish folk epic, the *Kalevala*, as something of a benchmark for ancientness: 'the Celts, though they had less of the old ways than the makers of the *Kalavala*, had more of it than the makers of the sagas.'[34] Clearly, in the league table of primitive insight, the Finns, for Yeats, were number one.

Though he was surely inspired by the 1888 English translation of the *Kalevala*, it is also likely that Yeats's appreciation for Finland as a distinctive source of European culture – neither Slavonic nor Scandinavian but poised between East and West – was the result of his cosmopolitan involvement in contemporary art movements. In the 1890s, Finland was entering a period of creative ferment, especially in painting. Absorbing the lessons of French symbolism, Finnish artists such as Akseli Gallen-Kallela, Pekka Halonen and Väinö Blomstedt were forging a new pictorial language based on explicitly national themes. Their work was celebrated and displayed in the great metropolitan centres of European cultural power.

For centuries a province of Sweden, Finland had become a Russian Grand Duchy in 1809. The nineteenth century had seen a growing movement among Finnish elites towards the cultivation of a distinctive

Rowan as folklore emblem: Finnish stamp celebrating the 150th anniversary of the *Kalevala*. It depicts the poet-singer Larin Paraske, 'The Finnish Mnemosyne', who could recite some 32,000 folkloric verses from memory.

and separate national culture. Artists and intellectuals, most of them raised with Swedish as a first language, deliberately adopted the Finnish language spoken by the peasant majority, seeking to promote it as a vector of patriotic solidarity. The *Kalevala*, an epic crafted from folk materials gathered in remote Karelia by Elias Lönnrot, was pivotal in inspiring commitment to this cultural mission. Not only did it prove that Finnish could be the vehicle for a distinctive and distinguished poetry, but it seemed to open a window onto authentically Finnish lifeways and to primitive spirituality still surviving in rural regions. For the painters, illustration of narrative episodes from the *Kalevala* provided an opportunity to combine patriotic investment in landscape with sympathetic ethnographic realism: the 1890s saw a sudden flowering of artworks inspired by the poem – and one of the most famous, Akseli Gallen-Kallela's *Kullervo Cursing* (1899), makes rich symbolic use of the rowan.

Gallen-Kallela's painting depicts a fraught moment in the story of the *Kalevala* character Kullervo, a potent source of nationalist symbolism in Finnish literature and music: in 1892, Jean Sibelius had premiered his *Kullervo* symphony, hailed in the Helsinki press as 'the first living Finnish musical work'.[35] In the episode chosen by the painter, Kullervo, whose whole tribe was obliterated in war, leaving him exiled and estranged, has been reduced to serfdom. He is working as a herdsman in the summer pastures, protecting the cattle from wild animals as they forage in the forest. His mistress, however, bakes a rock into his bread, causing him to snap his cherished knife, the only heirloom of his lost kin. Kullervo curses the mistress, taking vengeance by summoning wolves and bears to hunt and kill her. In the painting, the crumpled knife is visible at Kullervo's belt. His dog, a

Pekka Halonen, *Rowan Tree*, 1908, oil on canvas. The late 19th century saw a revival of nature-inspired visual culture in Finland.

Finnish spitz, sniffs at the stony loaf as Kullervo brandishes his fist in the direction of the village, grimacing. The cattle are just visible in the background, wandering out of frame as storm clouds gather on the wild horizon. A rowan holds its berries, halo-like, above the hero's racked visage.

What are we to make of Gallen-Kallela's choice of this particular scene, his careful rendering of the rowan? It is usual to note, first of all, that the 1890s was a period of increased Russification in Finland, with many nationalists interpreting the creeping extension of Russian bureaucratic powers as a threat to the nominally autonomous status of the region. *Kullervo Cursing* was immediately received as a powerful symbol of Finnish defiance during the so-called 'period of oppression'. It was taken, in particular, to encapsulate the nationalism of the Young Finns – a cultural and political movement of which Gallen-Kallela was a prominent member.[36]

Yet the painting is more than just a thinly veiled representation of anti-Russian sentiment. The painting's composition gestures towards more fundamental concerns, especially in the framing of landscape elements, kept starkly separate from the foreground action by a rock and a screen of fallen trees. Straddling this threshold, Kullervo's rowan marks a charged division between nature and culture. It is poised like an ambassador from the wilds hidden in the depths of the scene; Kullervo, whose own spindly frame is a deliberate rhyme for the tree, is acting as its spokesperson.

So what, through Kullervo, does the rowan have to say? It should be noted, first of all, that the painting's vantage – as if the viewer has reached the edge of civilization – is characteristic of Finnish landscape works from the early 1890s.[37] Many, such as Gallen-Kallela's own *The Great Black Woodpecker* (1893), present the view from the raised aspect of a cliff, with impassable forest beyond. In Väinö Blomstedt's 1898 canvas *Sunset*, we are brought to the edge of a lake; a rowan stands at the threshold of the visionary place, its infinite horizon. Implicit in

Akseli Gallen-Kallela, *Kullervo Cursing*, 1899, oil on canvas.

such imagery was a desire to celebrate and protect a wild region as yet untouched by modernization and to frame it as a source of authentic culture. In Blomstedt's painting, the lake-isle is a microcosm of primordial Finland, a timeless otherworld to which the rowan offers emblematic access.

More than a Romantic idealization of wilderness, such imagery had its origins in genuine political exigencies. The 1890s saw an enormous growth of industrial forestry in Finland. By 1900, despite having a tiny population, the region controlled around 10 per cent of the world's exports of sawn goods.[38] The sale of forested land by small farmers, its consolidation into larger corporately owned units, was an engine of modernization and of demographic change, as agricultural labourers – like Kullervo in the painting – were proletarianized. For modernizers, forestry would give Finland the wealth to command independent statehood. But at what cost? The environmental argument implicit in the framing of Romantic landscapes was also a political provocation. Was 'Finnishness' to be achieved by a vision that saw the land as a resource and an engine of commodification?

In *Kullervo Cursing*, the single rowan in the foreground adds texture to this question. While Gallen-Kallela depicts the background woods as unbroken stands of spruce and pine, the very vision of a uniform 'resource', his contrasting attention to the rowan, argues for something sacred encapsulated in the diversity of the ecosystem. Essentially a nuisance weed to loggers, in Gallen-Kallela's handling, the rowan becomes a cipher of natural beauty and biodiversity, impossible to price. The implied ethical lesson – to see clearly, to cherish the detail – is embodied in the painting's composition. The rowan is sited with an ecological sensitivity that suggests sustained *plein-air* attention. In boreal forests, rowan grows where trees have fallen, letting light in from the canopy. Here, fallen logs, an important aspect of woodland biodiversity often removed by foresters, appear to protect it from browsing by herbivores. A double for Kullervo himself, the tree is a symbol of survival and potential renewal.

Väinö Blomstedt, *Sunset*, 1898, oil on canvas. The painting captures rowan's ecological preference for forest edges and its reputation as a threshold to mysterious otherworlds.

The rowan's meaning is also enriched by knowledge of the painting's source. In the *Kalevala* text, Kullervo's broken knife is preceded by one of the most extraordinary moments in the whole epic. Preparing him for service, his mistress makes an incantation, invoking protection for her animals. She asks the forest spirits to spare them – for bears and wolves to keep at bay – and conjures a vision of plenty flowing from the growing forest to the human community. The whole performance gives us a vision of an idealized yet tense arrangement between the wilderness and the culture clustered at its edges. 'Let us make a pact,' the mistress chants, 'settle our border dispute/ for our lifetime, for our world/ . . . for all our days.' The rowan, tree of protection, is invoked as one of the guarantors of this pact: 'make the willow a herdsman/ an alder a cow-watcher/ a rowan a keeper.'[39]

Such settlement with the wild, for which the rowan is a crucial intermediary, is envisioned in the *Kalevala* as the source of communal justice: it defines the bounds of reciprocity and the sustainable sharing of wealth. When she betrays her serf by adulterating his bread – a classic infringement of the worker's natural right – the mistress dishonours the very compact she so performatively enacts: it is therefore fitting that Kullervo summons the wolves and bears for his vengeance. In the painting, Kullervo is primed to invoke such powers, but they have not yet come to wreak their havoc. The cattle are at his back. They forage on in the glade, oblivious, arrested in a moment of latency. It is not quite right, then, to say that Kullervo is standing at a barrier to the wild. Rather, he presides over a brief interval of ideal reconciliation between nature and culture; neither wild nor cultivated, its custodial spirit is the rowan.

In Gallen-Kallela's treatment, Kullervo is more than a symbol of anti-Russian defiance. His skinny torso, the trousers barely gripping his waist, embodies the betrayal of the ordinary rural worker when lands are sold for rapid profit. Yet, like the rowan, which is his double, he is also an emblem of vitality and natural expressivity. Gallen-Kallela's painting is a remarkable condensation of the symbolic richness of the rowan in cultural-nationalist discourse. Uniting the aesthetic and folkloric with an underlying feeling for the practical and ecological, it offers a genuine sense that the question of national self-definition must begin with the relationship between human economies and the health of the environment. It is from this interaction that, throughout its history, the rowan has drawn its most potent meanings – it is an interaction we continue to explore in the following chapter.

four
Romantic Ecologies

❧

O
n 28 July 1853, incessant rain abating and fresh canvas
having just arrived from London, the painter John Everett
Millais and art critic John Ruskin finally walked out to
their pre-agreed location.[1] They had arrived at Brig O'Turk, in the
Trossachs, a few weeks earlier, the last stop on a Scottish tour designed
by Ruskin to awaken his young Pre-Raphaelite protégé to the pre-
eminent beauty of mountain scenery. Ruskin and his neglected wife,
Effie, were staying in 'a Highland cottage . . . just under Ben Ledi', and
it was only a short distance uphill from their front door to the pre-
cipitously rocky course of the River Turk, where Ruskin would stand
for his portrait.[2] Though near, the site was not easy to access, requiring
that the party scramble down a steep bank of rock, slick with spray
and mazy with scattered vegetation. 'Millais has fixed on his spot,'
Ruskin wrote in a letter to his father, 'a lovely piece of worn rock, with
foaming water . . . and a noble overhanging bank of dark crag.' In
another letter, he described the 'beautiful piece of Torrent bed' as a
kind of bower 'overhung with honeysuckle and mountain ash'.[3]

It was one of these pioneering rowans, emerging perpendicular to
the forbidding brow of gneiss that dominates the upper half of the
canvas, that provided Millais with a starting point for the work.[4]
Defying approaches to portraiture established in the High Renaissance
– figures painted first, the landscape an accessory and largely conventional presence – Millais began with a quick reference sketch of Ruskin,
marking out the composition before embarking on a painstakingly

John Everett Millais, *John Ruskin*, 1853–4, oil on canvas.

detailed rendering of the circumambient ecology: a sputter of white lichen on spray-darkened stone; folds and strata of rock at Ruskin's feet, edges softened by time; a violet butterwort in the meagre soil of a crevice; and, most luxuriantly, water in all its turbulent variety – crizzled with foam at the convergence of flows, combed into glassy brightness as it rushes from a drop-off, crystal calm and flecked with reflections, the summer sky picked out in blue on beaded bubbles. The only things omitted were the clouds of midges.[5]

In the finished painting, the sapling rowan, though occupying a tiny area of the canvas, is painted with microscopic attention and given a remarkable compositional prominence. Boughs brightly lit against the baroque darkness of the stone, a terminal cluster of pinnate leaves, each picked out with pinpoint flecks of green and gold, hovers just above the subject's head. Offering both clarity of outline and a leap of colour against the umbrageous convexities of the 'dark crag', the tree has a practical as well as decorative purpose in the composition, serving as a reference point connecting the background with the putative outline of Ruskin's figure. By positioning it close to Ruskin's head, Millais maintained correct alignment as he set up his equipment for each new day of work. There were to be many.

As he worked its delicate form into chiaroscuro clarity, we can also imagine that Millais experienced the rowan as a marker of aesthetic commitment. Both he and Ruskin intended the painting to set a new standard of naturalism in art.[6] Ruskin, in particular, was determined that Millais, through a patient, almost worshipful, attention to living form, should achieve a degree of accuracy and finish, which would bring the act of representation into sympathy with nature's own processes. Not often required to pose, Ruskin was largely free to coax and goad the painter in his astonishingly tender labours. 'Millais is painting a picture of a torrent among rocks which will

Ruskin's sketch of the cottage he occupied with Effie at Glen Finglas, from a letter dated 16 October 1853. The site of the portrait is marked 'A'.

133

John Everett Millais, *Awful Protection against Midges*, 1853, pen and brown ink on paper.

While Millais painted, Ruskin had time to make his own drawings of the landscape and its plants: John Ruskin, *The Rocky Bank of a River, c.* 1853, pen and brown ink and graphite on paper.

make a revolution in landscape painting,' he wrote elatedly in October, as if he had forgotten it was also to be his portrait. 'I have stopped all this time to keep [him] company – to keep him up to the Pre-Raphaelite degree of finish.'[7] Ruskin's exalted expectations started with the rowan: 'my portrait is verily *begun* today and a most exquisite piece of leafage done already, close to the head – the finest thing I ever saw him do.'[8]

In one minor sense at least, Ruskin was quite right about the revolutionary nature of Millais's painting: at the end of a week's labour, that 'exquisite piece of leafage' was the first recognizable rowan tree in a major British painting. Though little more, at first sight, than a gorgeous miniature, Millais's rowan is thus of considerable art-historical importance. An index of epochal shifts in landscape aesthetics, it unites Pre-Raphaelite affection for natural detail with an appreciation for wild scenery which, having its roots in Romanticism, had reached a pitch of spiritual intensity in Ruskin's own writings.

This chapter takes Ruskin's portrait as a springboard for reading the presence of rowan trees in Romantic literature and painting, arguing that appreciation for the species is a marker of shifting attitudes to natural beauty. Unlike oak or willow, rowan is not a tree with particular prominence in 'canonical' art and literature before the late eighteenth century. Unmentioned by Shakespeare, Milton, Pope – absent, even, from the work of proto-Romantic figures such as Cowper and Gray – literary appearances of rowan are mostly confined, before the celebrated writings of the English Lake Poets William Wordsworth and Samuel Taylor Coleridge, to marginalized forms such as folksong, ballad and Celtic myth.

In 1802, however, Coleridge channelled his own experiences of walking in the Lakes into a vision of the exiled Romantic lover. It is a rare and early mention of the rowan as a guardian spirit of Romantic inspiration:

> Sweet breeze! thou only, if I guess aright,
> Liftest the feathers of the robin's breast,
> That swells its little breast, so full of song,
> Singing above me, on the mountain-ash.[9]

Wordsworth, too, would give the tree symbolic importance in his long poem *The Excursion*. Characteristically feminine, it also serves the poet as a figure for the mutually beneficial interchange of nature and humanity:

> The Mountain-ash
> No eye can overlook, when 'mid a grove
> Of yet unfaded trees she lifts her head
> Decked with autumnal berries, that outshine
> Spring's richest blossoms; and ye may have marked,
> By a brook-side or solitary tarn,
> How she her station doth adorn: the pool
> Glows at her feet, and all the gloomy rocks
> Are brightened round her. In his native vale
> Such and so glorious did this Youth appear.[10]

Notably absent from 'high' art before the nineteenth century, rowan claims its place, here, in the ecology of Romantic art. It is an intriguing indicator of the politics of landscape aesthetics at the dawn of the industrial age.

As his Ruskin portrait took shape, the rowan offered Millais's eye a haven of outline among the bewildering beauty of Scottish rock and torrent. In this respect alone, the painting adds to the tree's long-standing association with domestic refuge in the wild. But might there be more particular meanings at work in the painted tree?

The Victorians, it is worth remembering, were particularly invested in botanical symbolism, a trait signally evident in the so-called 'Language of Flowers', an arbitrary code in which each bloom was assigned symbolic meanings entirely abstracted from ecological reality.[11] In early works such as *Isabella*, moreover, Millais had made a point of marrying vivid naturalism to dense emblematic allusion, alerting his audience to the symbolic function of background plants by placing them directly above the heads of his protagonists, just as he does with Ruskin's rowan.[12] We can assume, then, that the botanical elements of Millais's painting, especially those placed closest to the central figure, will be saturated with meaning. But of what sort?

In nineteenth-century portraits, it was common for background landscapes to be used symbolically, alluding to public conceptions of the sitter.[13] However, Millais's painting, I'd argue, takes this a step further, using the ambient ecology to propose a detailed homage to Ruskin's ideas about nature and art. The carefully composed rowan can be seen as central to this purpose, acting as a charged passage between inner and outer realities. Limbs reaching out, as if to touch the critic's head, it implies a visual rhyme for the famous hand of Adam in the Sistine Chapel. Ruskin had seen Michelangelo's work in person, and Millais would have known it from copies used for academic exercises at the Royal Academy. Whether deliberate or not, the echo is illuminating. For if Michelangelo used the anticipated touch of fingers to signify Adam's incipient animation with divinely inspired life, Millais's painting surely evokes a similarly spiritual sense of the inter-penetration of mind and the materials of nature. Though his posture suggests he is gazing downstream, Ruskin's eyes, when examined closely, are softly illuminated, almost glazed. His hair and face are lit with a beatific glow. The effect is an intimation of intense and

Millais often placed symbolic plants directly above the heads of his figures. In this detail from *Isabella*, 1848–9, the rose and passion flower are emblems of constancy and suffering.

visionary inwardness, as if the painting were the record of a moment of sudden insight and feeling.

What would Millais have known about Ruskin's ideas? At the time of the portrait, Ruskin, at just 34 years old, was best known as the author of two volumes of *Modern Painters* and for *The Stones of Venice*, a compendious guide to the architecture of the Italian city. (The latter contained his remarkable essay on 'The Nature of Gothic'.) Though Ruskin and Millais's relationship soured – Millais fell in love with, and would eventually marry, Ruskin's long-suffering wife, Effie – the painting was begun in a spirit of admiration and mutual respect, an aura almost miraculously preserved in the finished work. During the initial phase of *plein-air* composition, in fact, Ruskin was preparing a set of lectures – on Turner, the Pre-Raphaelites and Gothic architecture – to be delivered in Edinburgh in the autumn; he discussed his ideas at length with Millais, who also helped him prepare illustrative plates. Millais's letters, too, suggest a sympathetic familiarity with Ruskin's writings; he had certainly discussed *Modern Painters* with his Pre-Raphaelite associate William Holman Hunt – a keen advocate of Ruskin's perspectives on art among the Brotherhood.[14]

Such respect went both ways. In 1851, Ruskin, already England's most revered and controversial critic, had publicly intervened to defend the Pre-Raphaelites from virulent attacks in the newspapers.[15] Ruskin and Millais were united in their rejection of academicism in art.[16] In *Modern Painters*, Ruskin had begun a spirited demolition of the prevailing standards of art-historical judgement of his era – standards that continued to inform the way art was taught in venerable institutions such as the Royal Academy.[17] Whereas most critics of the time praised work according to its degree of emulation of classical standards exemplified by the Old Masters, Ruskin set out to show that these very standards were the result of a decadence beginning with the major figures of the Italian Renaissance, notably Raphael.[18] For Ruskin, High Renaissance ideals had exerted such a powerful hold on subsequent artistic production that art had been led away from observation of nature and towards its own closed world of second-order vision. The result was a slide into conventionalism and excessive polish:

> the perfection of execution and the beauty of feature which were attained in [Raphael's] works . . . rendered finish of execution and beauty of form the chief objects of all artists; and thenceforward execution was looked for rather than thought . . . beauty rather than veracity.[19]

For Ruskin, it was J.M.W. Turner who had begun a revolution in artistic sensibility, returning painting to an earnest attempt to represent the truth of nature. Drawing on Ruskin's own years of devoted, scientifically informed attention to natural objects, the first volume of *Modern Painters* had offered a systematic demonstration of Turner's superiority to the Old Masters in the painting of every imaginable landscape feature: sky and clouds; mountains, rocks and soil; rivers, lakes and seas; foreground plants; close and distant trees – all, Ruskin showed, had gradually succumbed to the chimerical deformations of conventionalism; all had been restored to some degree of realism by Turner. 'We have too much picture-manufacturing,' he wrote,

> too much making up of lay figures with a certain quantity of foliage, a certain quantity of sky, and a certain quantity of water; a little bit of all that is pretty, a little sun and a little shade, a touch of pink and a touch of blue, a little sentiment and a little sublimity . . . all very neatly associated in a very charming picture.[20]

Ruskin trusted the Pre-Raphaelites precisely because their work, despite its evident naturalism and intense aesthetic commitment, was considered an offence to conventional standards of pictorial decorum and painterly elegance: it refused the accepted recipe for success for 'a charming picture'. In his 1851 pamphlet *Pre-Raphaelitism*,

Gaspard Dughet, *Mountainous Landscape with Approaching Storm, c.* 1638–9, oil on canvas.
In *Modern Painters,* Ruskin described the trees in classical picturesque paintings as
resembling parsnips or carrots.

Ruskin ranked Millais, with Turner, as 'among the few men who have
defied all false teaching', presenting a speculative depiction of Millais's
special perceptive powers, which uncannily predicts the Glen Finglas
portrait: '[He] sees everything, small and large, with almost the same
clearness . . . the leaves on the branches, the veins in the pebbles, the
bubbles in the stream.'[21]

Millais's painting of Ruskin repays this trust with the inclusion
of landscape elements – centrally the rowan tree – painted as if
designed to chime with Ruskin's aesthetic stipulations. Ruskin calls
for foreground rocks expressive of a geologist's eye for deep time,
for 'every crack and fissure' to exhibit 'the most delicious distinct-
ness': Millais surrounds him with them. Ruskin calls for falling water,
ornamenting 'every swell and hollow of the bed with [its] modulat-
ing grace': Millais frames him with such liquid beauty. Ruskin writes,
marvellously, of how, despite 'the constancy with which . . . leaves are
arranged on the spray . . . that regularity is modified in their actual
effect' so that the overall impression is of 'masses of illumined foliage,
all dazzling and inextricable, save here and there a single leaf on the
extremities': next to Ruskin's head, Millais picks out the exquisite

symmetries of the rowan's pinnate leaves; on the receding stem, he paints their diverse aspects as darker green vibrations of the air.[22]

Millais, in short, surrounds Ruskin with the emblems of his own visionary reinterpretations of natural beauty. The painting is both a wild scene and a kind of interior landscape. It encodes a mystical sense of identity between the self and nature, with the rowan occupying a central place as a conduit of this vision: the tree can be read both as transmitting illumination outwards from Ruskin's mind, infusing the artistic composition of the scene, and as blessing the critic's bowed head with powerful natural insight. Compositionally, the tree is an essential link in a circuit of sympathetic connections that starts from Ruskin's feet (emblem of his material embeddedness in the place), travels in a curve through the rocky outcrop at the left of the picture and then arches down through the rowan towards his lit brow, a cipher for his inward vision of reality.

It is especially appropriate that a rowan should take this role in the painting's symbolic economy. In his rather unhinged later work, *Proserpina*, Ruskin would propose his own anti-Linnaean taxonomy of the vegetable world, basing his groupings on his own eccentric moral schema. He made the rowan the type species of a genus he called the *Athenaïdes* – plants sacred to Athene, goddess of wisdom. 'The mountain ash,' he writes,

> in its hawthorn-scented flower, scarletest of berries, and exquisitely formed and finished leafage, belongs wholly to the floral decoration of our native rocks, and is associated with their human interests . . . not less spiritually, than the olive with the mind of Greece.[23]

Though this was written some two decades after the painting of his portrait, it is not impossible that he had the picture in mind – nor, indeed, that he had begun to formulate such ideas on the rowan during his Scottish tour. Either way, the tree becomes, for Ruskin, a symbol of sacred space and holy wisdom comparable to the olive

Ruskin's illustration of a
rowan leaf from *Modern
Painters*, vol. v (1885 edn).

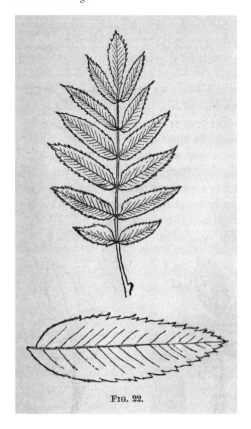

FIG. 22.

groves of the Acropolis. He was clearly moved by the beauty of the
rowan's form. In a gorgeous set of meditations on the morphology
of plant life, the section 'Of Leaf Beauty' in the fifth volume of *Modern
Painters*, Ruskin would use a drawing of its leaves to illustrate the
subtle asymmetry of pinnate leaflets, a clue to their identity as parts
of one ideal leaf. It is an apt emblem of his aesthetics: perfection as
the sum of imperfections – an idea, not a direct presence.

Whether or not Ruskin was voicing such thoughts to Millais in
the 1850s, his intense affection for each individual plant in its ecological specificity was already a source of energetic critical perception
in his writings. In his autobiography, *Praeterita*, he would render an
encounter with a tree as perhaps *the* decisive moment in his aesthetic
education:

Languidly, but not idly, I began to draw it; and as I drew, the languor passed away: the beautiful lines insisted on being traced . . . More and more beautiful they became, as each rose out of the rest, and took its place in the air. With wonder increasing every instant, I saw that they 'composed' themselves, by finer laws than any known of men. At last the tree was there, and everything that I had thought about trees, nowhere . . . 'He hath made everything beautiful, in his time,' became for me thenceforward the interpretation of the bond between the human mind and all visible things.[24]

As is especially evident in the above passage, Ruskin's mission for naturalistic art was infused with evangelical zeal. His early writings on art were characteristic of a time, before the full impact of Darwinism, in which scientific discovery was still routinely harmonized with religion.[25] Ruskin presented the artist as a prophet and teacher, restoring their contemporaries to proper joy in nature and, through this, to reverence for their fellow humans. Where art had slipped into decadence, this was a sure-fire sign of a society uprooted from its basis in a providential order: the judgement is there in the sardonic reference to 'picture-manufacturing' – academic painting, Ruskin implies, has been deflected from nature worship into the pursuit of profit, the artist enslaved by mechanistic, commercial formulae.

As Millais made his painting, the religious and social aspects of Ruskin's aesthetics were reaching a new pitch of clarity. In 'The Nature of Gothic', he had suggested that attention to architectural ornament could be used to diagnose the attitude of a society to its citizens and workers. Despotic or autocratic civilizations, Ruskin wrote, were characterized by the mechanical reproduction of certain stock forms, by repetitive patterns and the demand for a 'perfect' finish and symmetry in execution. Such demands stripped the craftspeople of initiative, training them, instead, in thoughtless, uninspired design. Ruskin explicitly compared this with the impact of factory work in Victorian England, arguing that perfection of the production process was worthless if it came at the expense of an individual worker's development and autonomy. More subtly, the criticism implies an analogy with the 'picture-manufacturing' of marketable painting. Both are evidence of distorted values, the individual made a victim of the social whole.

Instead, Ruskin valorized *imperfection* and *irregularity* of form. 'To banish imperfection is to destroy expression . . . to paralyze vitality,' he wrote, finding, in the abundant foliar embellishments of Gothic architecture, a cipher of social harmony:

> In that careful distinction of species, and richness of delicate and undisturbed organization, which characterize the Gothic design, there is the history of rural and thoughtful life . . . devoted to subtle inquiry; and every discriminating and delicate touch of the chisel, as it rounds the petal or guides the branch, is a prophecy of the development of the entire body of the natural sciences . . . the establishment of the most necessary principles of domestic wisdom and national peace.[26]

Again, Ruskin's words alert us to the symbolic depths of Millais's rowan. The tree is a natural manifestation of Gothic ornament. In his careful rendering of this irregular, crag-bound specimen, its form exemplary of a state of fragile and uncertain becoming, Millais channels the 'subtle inquiry' of the Gothic chisel, its 'delicate touch'.

Finally, Ruskin's work on Gothic was developed simultaneously with the most zealously evangelical expression of his nature worship – the second volume of *Modern Painters*. There, Ruskin laid out a biophilic sense of 'vital beauty', explaining how the appreciation of natural forms held ethical lessons essential to the health of society.[27] 'Throughout the whole of the organic creation,' he wrote, 'every being . . . is in its nature, its desires, its modes of nourishment, habitation, and death, illustrative or expressive of certain moral dispositions or principles.'[28] Most of all, Ruskin held, the right appreciation of nature could act as a kind of training in Christian charity and love of one's neighbour, a point sealed in a vision of ecological harmony, again curiously predictive of his own portrait:

> There is something, I think, peculiarly beautiful and instructive in this unselfishness of the Theoretic [imaginative] faculty, and in its abhorrence of all utility to one creature which is based on the pain or destruction of any other; for in such services as are consistent with the essence and energy of both it takes delight, as in the clothing of the rock by the herbage, and the feeding of the herbage by the stream.[29]

I began this section by noting how the rowan allowed Millais access to the wild scene, offering his eye a kind of home. We can now see that the rowan serves as a symbol of such refuge in a deeper and more spiritual sense, appealing to the inward eye. Its delicate beauty of form, its resilience and adaptability to 'clothe the rock', the care it elicits from the painter, all have their role in the symbolic economy of the composition as a compendium of Ruskinian thought: representing an ideal harmony between mind and world, Ruskin's rowan stands for the critic's profound belief in the essential benevolence of things, the foundation of a deeply Romantic vision of social hope.

Ruskin's vision of painting, at least in the 1850s, was in many ways the teasing out, in art-historical terms, of ideas first proposed in poetry – especially by the English Romantics. As if in acknowledgement of this imaginative debt, Ruskin had used an epigraph from Wordsworth's poem *The Excursion* on the title pages of both published volumes of *Modern Painters*. In the finished, five-volume work, Wordsworth is mentioned more than any other poet.[30] Although Ruskin is unlikely to have known it, it is a nice historical coincidence that, precisely fifty years before his own trip to Glen Finglas, Wordsworth, along with his sister, Dorothy – with whom, despite his recent marriage, he still lived at Dove Cottage in Grasmere – and their friend Coleridge, had also travelled to the area.

By that time, Loch Lomond and the Trossachs were already acknowledged as a gateway to the Highlands, welcoming a growing stream of tourists ready to enthuse over mountainous and pictur-esque landscapes.[31] The veneration of such wild places was a relatively new phenomenon in the West. For centuries, in fact, mountains had been considered in Christian nations as, at best, an inconvenient interruption of the fertile pastoral lowlands and, at worst, a refuge for all kinds of spiritual and social evils – demons and dragons, sav-ages and brigands.[32] In the eighteenth century, though, such attitudes had begun to shift. Pioneering writers such as Horace Walpole and Thomas Gray returned from visits to the Alps, extolling the fearful abysses and wastes of ice as evidence of God's most terrifying aspects – a kind of Old Testament supplement to the benevolence exempli-fied by natural beauty.[33] For these writers, fear and trembling, when safely managed, could be re-interpreted as reverence and religious awe, an idea given its most influential expression by Edmund Burke in his 1757 *Philosophical Enquiry* on the sublime.

The sublime, however, was not easily accessed in Britain and few could afford the expenditure of time or money required for travel to the Alps. With the invention of the picturesque, pioneered by writers such as William Gilpin, a happy medium was struck between the terrors of the sublime and the reassurances of the Beautiful. The picturesque had its origins in the enormous popularity, in Britain, of classical landscape painting of the seventeenth century, in particular the work of Claude Lorrain, Gaspard Poussin and Salvator Rosa – all artists whom Ruskin would later criticize in *Modern Painters*.[34]

At the heart of the picturesque was the cultivation of certain specialized habits of looking. To achieve a picturesque impression, viewers had to learn to position themselves so as to fit the landscape before them into classical modes of composition. By assuming an ele-vated vantage point, one might open a clear line to a distant, sublime horizon; preferably, a screen of trees would intervene on one side of the foreground, framing the distances and lending scale to some pastoral human figures; the intervening ground would be broken into planes of interest – with distant towns, hills, lakes and streams over which the eye could wander, imagining, with serene detachment, a culture peacefully integrated into the natural world.[35]

When the Wordsworths and Coleridge visited the Trossachs, they were already working out a new landscape aesthetic that subtly countered the dominant picturesque principles of their time – an effort in which the rowan plays an intriguing role.[36] On 7 September, four weeks into their tour, Dorothy and William reached the most northerly point on their itinerary, visiting the Falls of Bruar, a picturesque site that had been the subject of a 1787 poem by Robert Burns. Burns's poem ventriloquizes the mountain torrent of Bruar, imagining a petition to the local landowner:

> Would then my noble master please
> To grant my highest wishes,
> He'll shade my banks wi' tow'ring trees,
> And bonie spreading bushes.[37]

The 4th Duke of Atholl, John Murray, had heeded Burns's call, and when the Wordsworths arrived 'for the sake of Burns', they found the hillsides planted 'to a considerable height . . . with firs and larches intermingled' and criss-crossed with 'formal walks', a 'pleasure-path leading to nothing'.[38]

Dorothy's response to the scene is surprisingly condemnatory. 'Nothing could be uglier', she writes, than this contrived scenery. She and William 'wished that', rather than larches, the Duke had planted 'the natural trees of Scotland, birches, ashes, mountain-ashes'. The observation is characteristically ecologically astute and also tellingly anti-picturesque. Perhaps Dorothy was aware the larch had been introduced to Scotland by the Dukes of Atholl in the 1730s: the 4th Duke would plant some 15 million of the trees ('for profit and beauty'

View of the Falls of Bruar with larch plantation. Dorothy Wordsworth would be pleased to see the rowan in the left foreground.

– the order is telling), thus earning the nickname 'Planter John'.[39] For William, the planting of larches was a particular bugbear. He later referred to the tree as 'less than any other pleasing', a remark energized by his distaste for commercial forestry 'vegetable manufactory', he called it – in which the larch had begun to play a pre-eminent role. As a forestry tree, the larch was of particular use as material for fencing, a practice accelerated by the contemporary Enclosure Acts. In the early nineteenth century, forestry was amped up to provide timber for naval warfare against revolutionary France. Wordsworth's hatred for the larch, therefore, has important political resonances. Its presence signifies an attitude to the land characteristic of industrializing agriculture and the eradication of common rights; it is a marker of counter-revolutionary conservatism and imperialist military ambition.[40]

Dorothy, in her journal, similarly objects to the way the landscape is treated as a blank canvas for 'improvements' – tailored to the leisured eye rather than being seen as part of a regional ecology that included the lives and livelihoods of local people. The picturesque observer, as Dorothy knew, was trained to gaze on nature with an attitude of detached possession, transforming the landscape into a set of indifferent raw materials, ready to be rearranged for the pleasure and profit of the privileged. Because the picturesque was a pictorial grammar designed to subsume the particular into a universalizable pattern, it was largely unconcerned with the textures of local detail or the characteristics of species.[41] In a picturesque painting, a tree is an element of form, lending scale, curvature and a sense of depth to the scene. Dorothy's list of 'natural trees' laments this loss of particularity. To her mind's eye, the rowan's absence from the Falls of Bruar becomes an index of disconnection, of lost sympathy for the land and the people inhabiting it, for whom such trees held layers of association and meaning. Dorothy's rowan is an anti-larch, of no great economic value to landowners, yet richly indicative of emotional attachment to place.

This is not to say, of course, that some tree species were not of greater picturesque potential than others. Of special importance for picturesque foregrounds were gnarled and blasted oaks valued for their ruggedness of outline and suggestion of the ruinations of time. In the distance and middle distance, it was those trees that were monumental enough to act as a framing presence or to give a rugged grandeur to distant hillsides which were favoured. Because of its diminutive architecture, the rowan is a decidedly anti-picturesque tree, demanding, for proper appreciation of its charms, that we adopt a closer, more immersive view. For the connoisseur of picturesque landscape, it was therefore valued mainly for its colour. Indeed, in William Gilpin's brief remarks on the tree as an element of the picturesque, it is treated almost as an aspect of pigment, 'mixing' and being 'blended' with other more structural elements:

> There, on some rocky mountain, covered with dark pines and waving birch, which cast a solemn gloom over the lake below, a few mountain ashes joining in a clump, and mixing with them, have a fine effect. In summer the light green tint of their foliage, and in autumn the glowing berries which hang clustering upon them, contrast beautifully with the deeper green of the pines: and if they are happily blended, and not in too large a proportion, they add some of the most picturesque furniture with which the sides of those rugged mountains are invested.[42]

Such considerations were of particular importance to the architects of gardens, with the theory of the picturesque stimulating a revolution in landscape design. In fact, no other art form so aptly encapsulates the picturesque spirit in which, rather than art imitating nature, nature was expected to imitate art.[43] The scale of the works carried out at the great country estates was astounding, offering a concrete sense of the technological and logistical capacities that underpinned the picturesque attitude to landscape – an attitude that, in some sense, makes the picturesque garden an aesthetic complement to the rapid enclosure and agricultural intensification also being

carried out by landlords. At Chatsworth, an early masterpiece of
Capability Brown, some 15,000 specimens of rowan and birch were
transported for parkland planting in 1760 alone.[44] The very numbers
imply the way these trees were valued as an aggregate feature, to be
appreciated from a distance.

All of this adds context to our earlier observations on the single,
distinctly individual rowan in Millais's painting of Ruskin, as well as
to Dorothy's wounded sense of rowan's absence from the Falls of
Bruar. In both scenes, the tree stands as an index of immersive
encounter – of being *in among*, rather than outside or above, the natural world. Perhaps, in fact, as Dorothy imagined the rowan's presence
on the banks and hillsides of Bruar Water, she was also thinking back
to her own beloved Lake District, comparing the monotonous land-
scaping and circumscribed 'walks' with her own fell-edge garden at
Dove Cottage – the fence-less plot which, in her posthumously published journals, seems open, always, to free and pathless ramblings
in the hills.

In a characteristic entry dated 23 April 1802, Dorothy records a
walk with William and Coleridge to Nab Scar:

[Coleridge] called to us and we found him in a Bower, the
sweetest that was ever seen. The Rock on one side is very high
and covered with ivy which was hung loosely about and bore
bunches of brown berries. On the other side it was higher
than my head. We looked down towards the Ambleside
vale . . . The Fir tree Island was reflected beautiful – we now
first saw that the trees are planted in rows. About this
bower there is mountain ash, common ash, yew tree, ivy,
holly[,] hawthorn mosses and flowers, and a carpet of moss
. . . We resolved to go and plant flowers in both these places
tomorrow.[45]

Here, too, the rowan is noticed and named as part of an organic
community of plants; again, it seems to mediate a sense of refuge

Trees at Chatsworth House, Derbyshire, with rowans well 'blended' into the hillside woods.

and safety, a reassurance of beauty in the midst of the sublime. Most revealing, however, is Dorothy's resolution to return and plant flowers at the bower. Unlike the picturesque, in which nature was to be grandly subsumed by artifice, Dorothy's vision places nature and culture in a more subtle relation of interpenetration and exchange; they are blended and confused – a deliberate contrast to the firs which, Dorothy suddenly notices, are 'planted in rows'.

Just as she brought flowers *out* to the mountains, Dorothy also gathered plants *in* to the garden at Dove Cottage. 'Dear Spot!' Wordsworth addresses the garden in a poem, 'whom we have watched with tender heed,/ Bringing thee chosen plants and blossoms blown among the distant mountains, flower and weed.'[46] Through such actions, the 'little nook of mountain ground' at Grasmere became a concentrated microcosm of the surrounding ecology, the distinction between 'flower and weed' – typically constructed around the demarcation of wild and cultivated space – deliberately blurred.[47] Indeed, just as she resolved to garden the bower, Dorothy also worked with William to construct a correspondent bower in the garden.[18] The rowan is present in a list of plants at Dove Cottage; in a later garden at Rydal Mount, Wordsworth planted rowans along the shaded walks where he declaimed his poetry.[49]

The rowan, then, was an important part of the complex ecology of the Wordsworthian mind – and thus of the development of English Romanticism and its environmental thought. This is true, not just in the sense that both William and Dorothy composed outdoors,

House and garden at Rydal Mount, Cumbria. The hillside walks were described as William Wordsworth's 'outdoor office'.

using bower and walk as sites of poetic contemplation and composition, but in the sense that the garden itself, as a place defined by slow and tender interchange between nature and culture, was the very image of the mutualistic, careful and, most of all, loving ecology that the Wordsworths were working to define in their writings.

In the final book of his long autobiographical poem, *The Prelude*, Wordsworth makes the connection explicit, using an extended analogy between Dorothy's gardening, her planting out of mountain bowers and its influence on his own aesthetics:

> But for thee, sweet Friend,
> My soul, too reckless of mild grace, had been
> Far longer what by Nature it was framed,
> Longer retained its countenance severe,
> A rock with torrents roaring
> . . .
> But thou didst plant its crevices with flowers,
> Hang it with shrubs that twinkle in the breeze,
> And teach the little birds to build their nests
> And warble in their chambers.[50]

For Wordsworth, Dorothy's influence saved him from a period in which, excessively fixated on the sublime, and on a correspondingly austere and heroic vision of politics, 'Nature . . . had fallen back' in his affections. And if Dorothy helped bring Wordsworth to new understanding of the natural world, then the rowan, one of the 'shrubs that twinkle in the breeze', a plant pointed out on the fells and planted in the garden, was integral to her teaching.

Such, then, is the place of rowan in the Romantic vision of ecology. Powerfully encapsulated in Millais's painted tribute to John Ruskin, it was a vision which emphasized the embeddedness of mind in world and encouraged a spirit of collaboration and interchange between nature and culture. Demanding that its audience be transformed by slow practices of loving attention, Romantic art teaches what Ruskin called 'powers of simple pleasure': rather than imposing ever-new demands of productivity and taste on the land, we are asked to abide with what there is.[51] 'THERE IS NO WEALTH,' Ruskin wrote, 'BUT LIFE.'[52]

Such a spirit continued to animate Millais's work long after his break with Ruskin. In 1874, he exhibited *Scotch Firs* at the Royal Academy, accompanying the painting with lines – 'the silence that is in the lonely woods' – which he attributed to Wordsworth, but are apparently an improvisatory misremembering of assorted poems. Though admired by the young Gerard Manley Hopkins, *Scotch Firs* again challenged its viewers.[53] It tantalizes, with a glimpse of distant sublimity, a violet cusp of hills. But the capacity to overlook, for the eye to escape its embeddedness, is denied: nature is *here*, where we are, crowding towards us, as if growing from the canvas. Refusing the convention of a wide and low vista, the scene is instead painted in the mode of a portrait, upright and narrow, with low evening sun flooding in, rich and amber, from the left. It is about the personality of a place, the receptive revelation of its uninterchangeable character. And there, on the right, a single characteristic leaf outlined against the dark fissures of the pine bark, is an old familiar, a talismanic sign – a whippy sapling rowan, waiting for light and opportunity.

A similar spirit is wonderfully at work in the contemporary paintings of Ivan Shishkin, one of a clutch of great Russian landscapists of the nineteenth century and the first to attach a central importance to *plein-air* study.[54] Few artists have given such concentrated attention to the naturalistic depiction of forests. In a succession of paintings from the 1870s, Shishkin frames a near-impenetrable density of bosky texture, a vision of bewildering and apparently disordered presence – toppling firs, mossed stones, shallow fragments of water, a dense clitter of fallen wood – which enact a near-total refusal of the eye's desire for transcendence or escape.[55] Among the most successful realizations of this vision is *Birch and Rowan* (1878), a painted sketch of

John Everett Millais, *Scotch-Firs: 'The Silence that Is in the Lonely Woods',*
1873, oil on canvas.

the forest's edge – or perhaps a clearing – in which the thick vib-
ratory foliage of three sapling rowans emerges from a blanket of
murky brown shadow. Registered in a swarm of rapid brushstrokes,
marks that instantly convey the painter's sympathetic sense of shared
life, the trees leap out as tender emblems of the world's continual
emergence from nothingness.

Ivan Shishkin, *Birch and Rowan*, 1878, oil on canvas.

Having broken with the Academy of Arts in his native Russia, Shishkin had joined the democratic 'Itinerant' school. 'Hopefully a time will come,' he wrote, 'when all the broad expanses of Russia, alive and inspired, will gaze from the canvases of Russian artists.'[56] These words, which make the Russian landscape an embodiment of its people, imply a political subtext informing *Birch and Rowan*. The painting imbues nature with an emblematic connection to the lives of Russian workers and serfs – struggling under autocratic rule but, like opportunistic rowans at the forest edge, awaiting their moment in the sun.

It is to Russia – and revolution – that we turn next.

В ЭТОМ ДОМЕ
С 21 ПО 31 АВГУСТА 1941 Г.
ЖИЛА РУССКИЙ ПОЭТ
• МАРИНА •
ЦВЕТАЕВА
РУС ШАГЫЙРЕ
1941 ЕЛНЫҢ 21-31 АВГУСТЫНДА
БУ ЙОРТТА ЯШӘДЕ

Rowan sculpture and memorial plaque at the Tsvetaeva Memorial House Museum, Yelabuga, Russia.

five
Other Russias

It is hard to write about the twentieth century without resorting to cliché. 'The age of extremes', the historian Eric Hobsbawm called it. It was a century of global warfare and genocide, of revolution and national liberation, of utopian hope and savage disillusionment. It was a century in which ceaseless technological invention – advances in medicine, agriculture, communications, media, travel – went hand in hand with an exploding, increasingly urban, global population. It was a century in which the possibility of plenty was compromised by rising inequality and unprecedented ecological spoliation.

Already, for the German writer Walter Benjamin, the first decades of the 1900s seemed to signal an era of such upheaval that experience would become ever-more meaningless as a source of wisdom. 'A generation that had gone to school on a horse-drawn streetcar', he wrote, in a much-quoted description of the First World War, found itself 'under the open sky in a countryside in which nothing remained unchanged but the clouds, and beneath these clouds, in a field of force of destructive torrents and explosions, was the tiny, fragile human body.'[1] It is a tender, prophetic image of the individual at the mercy of objective social forces.

For Benjamin, a Marxist, the war was a direct result of the contradictions of capitalist society. A battle for competitive advantage between national factions of the European bourgeoisie, it slipped the mask from a terror lurking beneath the very condition of 'progress'.

Capitalist society, Marx had predicted, would be characterized by 'constant revolutionising of production, uninterrupted disturbance of all social conditions, everlasting uncertainty'.[2] The war was that, sped up to bullet speed.

While Benjamin reacted with horror, for Vladimir Lenin, writing from exile, the war was an urgent political opportunity. This 'mighty accelerator', he argued in *Pravda* in March 1917, had already led to the overthrow of the Romanovs; once the people realized that the new bourgeois provisional government had no intention of leaving the conflict, it would also sweep the Bolsheviks to power.[3]

When the Bolsheviks did seize office, in October that same year, they found themselves presiding over a vast, decentralized and largely peasant nation. While other leftist parties argued that Russia needed

Lone rowan near the medieval town of Suzdal, Russia. For 20th-century writers and artists, the rowan often symbolizes the dignity of the individual life.

a period of bourgeois government to develop economically – creating the conditions for an eventual proletarian utopia – Lenin's Bolsheviks saw the revolution itself as a way of keeping their foot on the historical accelerator. They set out to create, by force and decree, an economic and cultural transformation to match and exceed that of capitalist nations.[4]

In some sense, the experience of revolutionary Russia can be seen as a grotesque microcosm: an image of the century as if viewed in a fairground mirror. In both this chapter and the next, we look at how twentieth-century artists and writers have used the rowan in explorations of political and personal upheaval – of displacement, exile and bewildering social change – which were characteristic of their time.

The rowan, as we have seen, is a plant whose limited economic value gives it a counter-utilitarian resonance tied to the aesthetic. Extending the Romantic symbolism of the tree, the works explored in these chapters propose the rowan as an emblem for the dignity of the individual person – and for modes of value and experience either unassimilable to the logic of economic development or invisible to the materialist rationality of modern science. For Russian writers Marina Tsvetaeva and Boris Pasternak, subjects of the present chapter, such meanings allowed the rowan to serve as the threshold to an alternative, counter-factual Russia: an imaginary, yet very real refuge from the economistic autocracy established – murderously – in the decades of Stalinization.

In writing that places an emphasis on vulnerability and isolation, the choice of a rowan as a talisman makes compelling ecological sense: try re-reading Benjamin's description of the battlefields of the First World War, but picture, this time, a single fragile rowan in the midst of the blasted landscape, alone under a vast sky. It is an image that has an evocative connection to the life of Marina Tsvetaeva, one of the great poets of the twentieth century. Most of all, it encapsulates a sense of ambivalent singularity, of something standing alone, both dignified and abandoned, autonomous and subjected. Such was the destiny that Tsvetaeva came to see as her particular fate as a poet. On 31 August 1941, two years after returning to Russia from nearly twenty years of exile and wandering — of fervent yearnings channelled into poetry, letters and a series of love affairs — Tsvetaeva hanged herself in a rented room in the small city of Yelabuga. Evacuated east to escape the German forces who were rapidly advancing on Moscow, she had arrived there only ten days earlier. Penniless and abandoned, she was buried in an unmarked grave.[5]

In the twenty-first century, you can visit the house without moving from your chair. I open Google Maps and zoom out from Paris, where Tsvetaeva lived in exile from 1925 to 1939. Europe resolves into a jig-saw of borders, names of cities melting into a satellite patina of greens and greys. At this virtual distance, nations seem strangely jumbled — as if just spawned, by some ongoing mitosis, from the vast unpar-celled landmass to the east. Just to locate its name, 'Russia', you have to drag the map until Mongolia and China are at the centre of the picture. Looking like nothing but empty steppe, forest and tundra, the sense of sudden space hits with a dart of existential angst.

I move in closer. Moscow appears, and I scroll east to where the Tatar city of Kazan lies wrapped around a wide right-angled bend of the Volga. South of Kazan, the Volga bulges like a python where it swallows up another too-big river — the Kama. I trace these waters east past Chistopol until — finally — Yelabuga. A bit of zooming and scrolling, and I drop the faceless avatar into Street View at the inter-section of Malaya Pakvrovskaya and Kazanskaya. A hundred-yard click north, and there it is, on the right, a modest single-storeyed timber house. The whole geographic arc of a life, a life that tracked the historic upheavals of half a century, reduced to a seated minute.

On the corner of the house, there is a small plaque, just legible in the image. For ten days in August 1941, the text confirms, 'Russian poetess' Marina Tsvetaeva stayed here. Planted on a thin strip of lawn out front, a tall, compact rowan is arrested in eternal late-summer, berries just forming, leaves a thickened green. In earlier photos, the

Rowan planted outside the Marina Tsvetaeva Memorial House Museum, Yelabuga.

rowan is not yet there. It must have been planted later, a living tribute: all around the city, cast-iron rowan sculptures mark memorial sites to the poet.

> The rowan tree flared
> in a cluster of red.
> Trees were shedding their leaves
> I came into the world

This is how she referred to her birth (26 September 1892) in a poem of 1916.[6] The rowan is offered as a double for Tsvetaeva's poetic gift: a mischievous, untimely force, a flaring energy, counter to the ordinary direction of things.

The rowan is a consistent and remarkable presence in Tsvetaeva's oeuvre. Figured, in her pre-exile poems, as a kind of second-self, it would later become her beacon of an inner Russia, a nation lived through displacement. Tsvetaeva's departure from the country, in May 1922, was typical of many emigres – her return, in June 1939, far less so. In the wake of the October Revolution, her husband, Sergey Efron, had fought for the White Armies at the Don, fleeing, at their eventual

Memorial sculpture to Tsvetaeva in Tarusa, Russia. A rowan sprig from a nearby tree has been placed in her hand.

defeat, via Constantinople to Prague. With Efron away, Tsvetaeva fought her own battles, living and writing through the fevered release, the chaos and penury of revolutionary Moscow.[7] For most of these years, Tsvetaeva had no idea of Efron's whereabouts. When she finally received news of his escape, she was able to get papers to leave Russia with their daughter, Ariadna, travelling to Berlin before joining Efron in Czechoslovakia. In the exiled years that followed, both remained attached by links of intense, almost-spiritual affection to their homeland.

Tsvetaeva was suspicious of this nostalgia, which she knew could be exploited for political purposes. Her 1934 poem 'тоска по родине' (*Toska po Rodine*) goes to the heart of this ambivalence. The poem itself is untitled, with the heading taken from its opening line, a phrase variously translated as 'Homesickness', 'Longing for the Motherland' and 'Yearning to get back home'.[8] The historian Svetlana Boym places the word *toska* among an international lexicon of 'untranslatable' terms for nostalgic longing – each, in its specificity, enacting the nostalgist's claim to cultural uniqueness: 'The whispering sibilants of the Russian *toska*, made famous in the literature of exiles, evoke a claustrophobic intimacy,' she writes, a 'crammed space from where one pines for the infinite'.[9]

Tsvetaeva's poem begins by scoffing at such longing: 'Yearning to get back home! Obscure/ complaint I unmasked long ago.' In subsequent verses, such performative scepticism gives way to a self-lacerating vision of inevitable displacement, a crescendo of grim humour. The poet is a 'captive lion', a 'Kamchatkan bear without/ an ice flow'; 'I don't care which [language] people fail to understand me in,' she goes on, 'gobbling up . . . newspapers,/ milking gossip . . ./ The twentieth century is theirs – my habitat's all centuries!'[10] Being in the infinite, it seems, is precisely the problem.

The poem is a startling condensation of Tsvetaeva's later themes: her scorn for materialism and the greed of contemporary life; her tragic–heroic sense of the poet, doomed to misunderstanding and abandonment. Reflecting on political exile, she finds it brings into focus a more fundamental condition of spiritual displacement. It is a vision with deep roots in European Romanticism.[11]

At the end of the poem, however, something strange happens – an unexpected detonation in memory: 'Yet should I happen on a bush,/ especially a rowan tree . . .' Here, determined renunciation fades into introspective silence; the reader is abandoned on the brink of a Proustian reverie for which no words can be conjured by the poet. It is as if, remembering the rowan, Tsvetaeva uncovers a Russia not defined by public debate or newspaper politics. It is a place, I would suggest, that can only be mapped through the poet's intense investment in particular sense impressions: its geography, invisible to satellite and without continuous physical borders, is charted in the lyric interplay of poems, through subtle connections of imagery and sound.[12] As a materialization of this sensuous home place, Tsvetaeva's rowan haunts her poem, its susurrant leaves just faintly heard in the 'whispering sibilants' of that opening word – *toska*.

Writing 'Homesickness', Tsvetaeva was no doubt thinking back to the poem already mentioned – from the 1916 cycle *Poems about Moscow* – in which she claimed the rowan as a personal emblem. In May 1934, she had written to a friend that it was one of her 'favourite poems, the most *mine*'.[13] In that early lyric, too, it is the recurrence of sense impressions that gives coherence to a life, granting an idea of belonging – of a home located, somehow, in the pangs of the body, and the emotions grown from them:

> I feel even now
> the same urge to chew
> bright, bitter berries
> from the rowan tree.[14]

In these lines, Tsvetaeva seems to imply that she was born with a craving for the rowan's bitter fruit. Unable to settle for a sentimental distanced admiration, for an expected observation of the prettiness of the berries, she brings them close and breaks them open;

Modern matryoshka dolls with rowan berry decoration. Tsvetaeva's poetry resists
the sentimental association of rowan with motherhood.

she wants something powerfully inward and subjective, an invisible,
barely communicable tang – the flavour of poetry. Whereas for many
Russians the rowan was known as a tree of protection, a signifier of
normative femininity, for Tsvetaeva it serves as a cipher for her challenge to these norms, a symbol of risk and the acceptance of desire.
It is an emblem of political assertion and youthful optimism.

By the time of the lovely 1920s cycle *Trees*, written while Efron
and Tsvetaeva were living in a rural village outside Prague, much had
changed. In these poems, Tsvetaeva presents her rural life, lived on
the edge of mountain and forest, as one of withdrawal from urban
modernity into a realm of archetype and myth.[15] The first poem in the
cycle finds the poet 'having lost faith in those who die' and sick of
'duplicity in friends'.[16] She takes herself off like a prophet, 'aloft, where
rowan trees/ burn lovelier still than once King David'. The second

poem repeats the pattern: 'trees! It's your company I seek!/ Far from the maddening marketplace.'

Apostrophizing these montane forests, Tsvetaeva produces a catalogue of species ending with the rowan: 'mouth through which my psalms are sung: rowans, crammed with bitterness'. As it did in 1916, poetic language tastes of rowan berries. In exile, however, their bitterness is something altogether new: youthful confidence, the yearning for experience, becomes a record of the cost of speaking out, the pain of bearing witness to a bitter history. Yet a note of political hope remains in play: the hope that these verses – like the rowans, 'lovelier than . . . King David', whose beauty overwhelmed the tyrant Saul – will maintain an invisible kingdom, all of their own.

As much as she sought to build this inner home in poetry, thoughts of a return to Russia remained with Tsvetaeva throughout her exile. Perhaps she burned for one particular rowan: the tree that stood outside her childhood home on Moscow's Three Ponds Lane. Miraculously, when she returned to the Soviet Union, she found it still alive.[17] The discovery must have been a comfort, but the initiative for the homecoming was not her own. By 1931, Efron was involved in the 'Eurasian movement', a nationalist enterprise that claimed a special destiny for Russia, preaching return as a way to lead the country beyond Bolshevism. He applied to go back. To prove repentance of his counter-revolutionary involvements, Efron was recruited by the NKVD (the People's Commissariat for Internal Affairs, the interior ministry of the Soviet Union), operating undercover in France and probably co-opted into political murder. With his cover blown, he finally fled home in 1937, at the height of Stalin's purges. Tsvetaeva had little option but to follow. It was not long before both Efron and their daughter Alya were arrested and imprisoned, accused of spying for the Western powers. Tsvetaeva was left in an almost-impossible situation. Unable to publish under conditions of Soviet censorship, she was largely shunned by other writers – even to associate with her was a political risk. In August, she was evacuated, fatefully, to Yelabuga.[18]

Tsvetaeva's identification with trees, especially the rowan, was a lifelong preoccupation of her poetry and correspondence. Paradoxically, she seemed to feel they led her, in their reticent otherness, *towards* some truth about being human: 'Trees are so much like bodies you want to hug them, so much like souls . . . Impossible to tear oneself away'; 'concerning trees let me tell you, absolutely seriously, that every time someone I'm with notices – a *specific* [tree] . . . I feel flattered as if *I* were being loved.'[19] It was an enthusiasm she shared widely. To the poet and novelist Boris Pasternak – who had remained in the Soviet Union, and with whom Tsvetaeva felt an almost metaphysical kinship – she wrote, 'Go to the gods, to the trees! This isn't lyricism; this is medical advice.'[20]

The rowan, in fact, is so central to Pasternak's great achievement in prose, *Doctor Zhivago*, that I can only wonder whether the symbol was intended as a tribute to Tsvetaeva. Censored at home, *Zhivago* was first published outside the Soviet Union in 1957. The book's appearance left Pasternak embroiled in an international political controversy typical of the Cold War era: Party authorities denounced the book, but its author was awarded the Nobel Prize; knowing the risk of angering State authorities, Pasternak then had to refuse the honour. It is both a memoir of revolutionary Russia and a sprawling statement of political and spiritual views, which Pasternak had worked out over a lifetime's writing.[21]

With *Zhivago*, Pasternak set out to produce a *War and Peace* for the Soviet era. An epic Bildungsroman, the novel narrates the life of its hero, Yuri Zhivago, from orphaned childhood in *fin de siècle* Moscow, through medical service in the First World War, to the era of post-revolutionary Civil War. It projects the horrors of Stalinism back onto the days of Lenin's New Economic Policy.

Zhivago is also a love story. Throughout the narrative, Yuri's life is tied, by a thread of coincidence and increasingly spiritual intimacy, to that of the novel's heroine, Lara Guichard. They meet, fleetingly, in Moscow, then serve in the same military hospital. Later, they find each other in distant Yuriatin, a city in the Urals where Lara is left

Soviet rowan stamp,
1964.

abandoned by her husband, Antipov, now a general in the Red Army – he is the personification of revolutionary fervour, an anti-type for the novel's often-listless, dreamy protagonist. Yuri's love for Lara is central to Pasternak's philosophical response to Stalinization: it reaches its culmination in an encounter with a rowan in which the tree, as well as being intimately connected to the novel's heroine, is made the embodiment of certain mystic yet profoundly earthly qualities.

Central to Pasternak's project, and essential to understanding his symbolic use of the rowan in all its richness, is a difficult but visionary philosophy of *life*. Even his hero's name, Zhivago, translates as 'the living one'.[22] Pasternak's position, developed through extended dialogic encounters, is established early in the novel. First to lend it voice is the hero's uncle, Nikolai Nikolaevich. Committed to social reform, yet suspicious of any politics guided by a system of concepts, Nikolaevich lays out his own programme through a series of paradoxical provocations: 'I think we must be faithful to immortality, that other slightly stronger name for life. We must keep faith in immortality, we must be faithful to Christ!'

Life, immortality, Christ – the chain of equivalence is bewildering. And our perplexity only deepens when, declaring himself an atheist, Nikolaevich nevertheless states that Christ's crucifixion was the decisive moment in culture. It demonstrated, he states, 'that man does not live in nature but in history' and that 'love of one's neighbour' is the 'highest form of living energy'. 'The ancients did not have history,' he goes on, only 'the sanguinary swinishness of the cruel, pockmarked Caligulas . . . the boastful, dead eternity of bronze monuments and marble columns'.[23]

In Nikolaevich's speech, for all its gnomic eccentricity, we begin to grasp the main ingredients of Pasternak's singular thought, a secular religion of life built around a deeply personal and unorthodox interpretation of Christianity. For Pasternak, 'Christ' means divinity brought to earth – a recognition of the ordinary miracle of existence and the human charity that follows. In Christianity, he writes, godliness is rendered so 'emphatically human' that 'from that moment peoples and gods ceased and man began, man the carpenter . . . the tiller . . . the shepherd'.[24]

It was a humanist vision with risky political stakes. Nikolaevich's 'pockmarked Caligula' is unmistakeably a reference to Stalin, and the whole novel sets out to trace how the revolution betrayed the universalist promise that Pasternak saw as derived from Christianity: how it came to place objectified abstractions, 'monuments and marble columns', above the individual life, descending into terror, paranoia and inflexible ideology.[25] He was lucky to survive its publication.

In the novel's chronology, the revolution coincides with the first stirrings of Yuri's love for Lara, a moment of national and personal rebirth which he apostrophizes with feverish passion as a renewal of 'life'. For Yuri, however, as for Pasternak, the promise of social and personal renewal is swiftly betrayed. Kidnapped by Red Army partisans in the Urals and forced to serve as a doctor in the revolutionary war against Admiral Kolchak's Whites, Yuri finally experiences a moment of decisive disillusionment, expressing increasing frustration with 'the ideas of general improvement, as they've been understood since October'. 'I don't think the end justifies the means,' he complains, railing against the Marxist–Leninist 'remaking of life':

People who can reason like that . . . [have] never once known life . . . For them existence is a lump of coarse material, not yet ennobled by their touch, in need of being processed by them. But life has never been a material, a substance . . . it eternally alters and transforms itself, it is far above your and my dim-witted theories.[26]

At an encampment deep in the Siberian taiga, Yuri decides to desert the partisans. Just as he is sneaking away, he meets a sentry who questions him: 'I saw this rowan tree with frozen berries on it,' he answers, remembering a tree he had encountered some days before, 'I wanted to go and chew some.' When the sentry lets him pass, what follows is a moment rich with accumulated resonance. The rowan

was half covered with snow, half with frozen leaves and berries, and it stretched out two snowy branches to meet him.

Rowan berries in the snow. Exposure to frost tempers the harsh bitterness of the fruit.

Other Russias

He remembered Lara's big white arms, rounded, generous, and taking hold of the branches, he pulled the tree towards him . . . He was murmuring, not realising what he was saying, and unaware of himself.

'I shall see you, my beauty, my princess, my dearest rowan tree, my own heart's blood.'

The night was clear. The moon was shining. He made his way deeper into the taiga . . . dug up his things, and left the camp.[27]

Serving Pasternak as a living symbol, Yuri's rowan draws together many strands of the novel's argument. First of all, there is the Tsvetaevan urge to chew the berries, which the sentry immediately scoffs at as a 'squire's whim': 'three years we've been beating . . . it out of you,' he says, 'no consciousness'. Yuri's pointedly anti-utilitarian craving, which has nothing to do with nutrition, is offensive to the sentry's limited materialist sensibility. As with Tsvetaeva's yearning to taste the bitter berries, it signals commitment to a complex interiority, a measure of experience which cannot be captured by economic calculus.

For Pasternak, these longings are symbolic of life in its spontaneous unpredictability – of a feeling intimately connected with poetry. After his desertion, Zhivago rediscovers the ability to write: the novel ends with a sequence of symbolist lyrics calculated to represent an alternative biography of the hero. As with Tsvetaeva's sudden memory of the rowan, the inclusion of these poems makes the case that life's true value can never be measured or narrated. Neither a sum or sequence of achievements nor the accumulation of accolades or commodities, life, for Pasternak, resists the logic of consumerism and the curriculum vitae: it is a sense of deep joy associated with spontaneous states of mystical elation and profound existential pleasure. Finding its true home in the poem, life is manifested in powerful feeling: a taste of rowan berries and the unpredictable weave of secondary meanings – personal, historical, spiritual – which attach themselves to the flavour.

175

For Yuri, it is his intense love for Lara that re-awakens these beliefs, giving rise to an idealized relationship between the natural and human worlds, a connection that provides a basis for political change. As scholars have noted, Yuri's observations of nature are cumulatively expressive of the Russian Orthodox concept of *Sophia*, the wisdom of an ecstatic receptivity to the spirit associated with the Virgin Mary and with Christ's incarnation – it is an ideal that may preserve a trace of earlier cults, of peasant veneration for female nature divinities.[28] Marrying a mutualistic ecology to the spiritual idealization of motherhood, the rowan helps Pasternak envision the natural sources of a deeply Romantic and utopian communism:

> At the way out of the camp and the forest . . . there grew a solitary, beautiful, rusty-red-leafed rowan tree, the only one of all the trees to keep its foliage . . . Small winter birds, bullfinches and tomtits, with plumage bright as frosty dawns, settled on the rowan tree, slowly and selectively pecked the larger berries . . . Some living intimacy was established between the birds and the tree. As if the rowan saw it all . . . taking pity on the little birds, yielded, unbuttoned herself, and gave them the breast . . . 'Well, what can I do with you? Go on, eat, eat me. Feed yourselves.'[29]

In this description, the rowan is invested with the full force of Pasternak's desire for a political alternative to Stalinism – for a politics that would maintain the humanist fervour and levelling spirit of the revolution, while remaining true to his sense of life.

Profoundly personal, Pasternak's rowan is also a symbol with deep roots in Russian literature and lore. Since Pushkin, many Russian writers have drawn on folkloric ideas to dramatize a conflict of masculine and feminine archetypes in Russian culture: a tension between the patriarchal autocracy embodied by 'Father Tsar' and the health of 'Mother Russia', personification of the fertile earth and its peasant custodians.[30] Whereas the former represents a modernizing influence

Rowan and oak together. In Russian folk songs such as 'Slender Rowan Tree', these trees represent feminine and masculine archetypes.

with ties to the European Enlightenment, the latter preserves aspects of a matriarchal nature religion – the special preserve of folk custom and memory. When Father Tsar tyrannizes over Mother Russia – the old culture forgotten or dishonoured – the nation suffers. It is a populist motif that Pasternak deftly recapitulates, ironically placing the Soviet powers in the position of Tsarist authority.

There was also the legacy of Leo Tolstoy. In *War and Peace*, Tolstoy had chosen the oak as a talismanic tree central to his epic narrative. In a celebrated scene, Tolstoy's protagonist, Prince Andrei Bolkonsky, experiences a springtime epiphany as the leafing of an ancient oak coincides with his new love for Natasha Rostov. The moment is a

Slender Rowan Tree, album cover designed by E. Radkevitch for the state-owned Melodiya label, 1986.

spur to *public* deeds. To be loved by Natasha, Andrei must first achieve the patriotic glory of wartime sacrifice: 'all of them must learn to know me . . . that my life be not lived for myself alone.'[31] In placing the rowan – not the oak – at the centre of his novel, Pasternak announces his intention to exalt an alternative conception of the meaningful life.[32] Counterposed by the masculine oak, the rowan often serves as a feminine symbol in Russian folksongs: in 'The Slender Rowan', for example, it is an emblem of constancy and the sacrifices of motherhood. In opposition to Tolstoy's heroic sense of history, then – to his praise of great men and focus on action and visibility – Pasternak draws on folkloric symbolism of the rowan to celebrate invisible passion and the mysterious workings of human affection, a labour intimately connected with the emotional work of mothers.

Unlike Prince Andrei, Pasternak's 'hero' dies a nobody, living according to the obscure dictates of art. His, in the end, is a lyric rather than an epic morality – a vision of the good life resting on a belief in the importance of what George Eliot called the 'incalculably diffusive' influence of 'unhistoric acts'.[33] It is an ethics begging faith in some form of cosmic reconciliation. In a pivotal scene, Lara's husband, Antipov – the novel's embodiment of destructive Napoleonic willpower – is eventually betrayed by the Bolsheviks. When he shoots himself in desperation, his blood, 'rolled up with the snow', forms 'little red balls . . . like frozen rowan berries': in the moment of surrender, a glimpse of rebirth.[34]

Rowan growing over a moorland stream. Such rivers were often used for washing sheep, with stone washfolds built to keep the stock in place.

six

Uprootings

✣

In the previous chapter, we saw how the Russian writers Boris Pasternak and Marina Tsvetaeva evoked the rowan in their deeply personal reckonings with revolutionary change. For many other twentieth-century artists, the rowan has served as a measure of slower yet equally significant processes of uprooting and upheaval.

In the 1930s, the Northumbrian modernist Basil Bunting published a number of short lyrics voicing a sense of injustice at the displacement of rural populations. In 'The Complaint of the Morpethshire Farmer', a poem strongly influenced by the modern ballads of Wordsworth and Burns, Bunting imagines overhearing a farmer on a train platform in Morpeth. Faced with the prospect of emigration to Canada, the poem's speaker laments the slow ruin of his land and livestock, the marks of habitation gradually erased. Picturing his flock displaced to 'other braes', his painted brand fading from their fleeces, he goes on to recall the upland burn where he would have washed them in previous seasons:

> The fold beneath the rowan
> where ye were dipt before,
> its cowpit walls are overgrown.[1]

Historically, as Bunting's own notes make clear, the economic impulse behind the farmer's distress was the tendency for large landowners to pressure tenants into leaving their pastoral farms. Letting the land

Mixed woodland of birch, alder and rowan on the track to the cleared village of Hallaig, Raasay.

revert to bare heather moor, they could make more money selling the experience of driven grouse shoots than from agricultural rents.[2] 'Sheep and cattle are poor men's food,' the farmer bitterly notes, 'grouse is sport for the rich.' The poem's rowan is a melancholy sign of faded human presence, of forgotten practices and beliefs. Growing over a stone washfold, where sheep were gathered to have their fleeces rinsed before going to market, the tree would once have been prized for its protective function, a charm against ill fortune for the livestock. In the farmer's forlorn vision of the future, the rowan has nothing but a ruin to guard.

If the plight of Northumbrian farmers is relatively little known, then the Highland Clearances have attained the status of an archetype of forced depopulation, revealing the blunt impact of market forces – and, where Gaelic-speaking populations were involved, racist pseudo-science – on the lives of rural workers. Born in 1911 on Raasay, a small island off Skye, the Gaelic poet Sorley MacLean paid particularly acute attention to the landscapes of clearance, grappling with an ambivalent attachment to the haunted – and haunting – beauty of emptied places. MacLean's life was profoundly marked by the history of evictions on Raasay. All four of his grandparents were removed from their farms in the nineteenth century, as dozens of families either emigrated or, making way for sheep in the greener south, were resettled in seaside crofts on the rocky northern fringes of the island.[3] Among the townships completely cleared – dwellings boarded up, stone walls left to crumble among bracken – were Hallaig and Screapadal, both well marked in the word map of MacLean's verse.

The woods of Raasay are unusually extensive, playing an essential role in the life of pre-clearance communities. After the Clearances, however, the island's previously well-managed woodlands were suppressed by grazing, slowly degenerating. During the Second World War, many were cut and replaced by conifer plantations, leaving only relics of older mixed woodland.[4] In his great lyric 'Hallaig' – first published in Gaelic in 1954 but quoted here in MacLean's own English translation – the poet transforms the entwined fates of Raasay's people and trees into a poignant music of loss and spectral return, of quiet rage and passionate longing. Witnessing the regeneration of birch woods on the island, and on the slopes above Hallaig, the poet animates the trees until they become a 'congregation of the girls' of Raasay, 'their laughter a mist in my ears,/ and their beauty a film on my heart'. Throughout the poem, the gregarious birch stands for the collective, for the joy of the communal, but when a particular person is intended, the poet narrows his focus to the rowan: 'my love is at the Burn of Hallaig . . . She is a birch, a hazel/ A straight, slender young rowan.'[5] As with Bunting's poem, this is a naming saturated with the pathos of history, its rowan a marker of lost lives, rituals no longer observed.

Similar histories are explored in the contemporary artist Andy Goldworthy's *Sheepfolds* project, a public artwork commissioned by Cumbria County Council in 1996. In consultation with local farmers, parish councils, schools and environmental agencies, Goldsworthy set out to transform derelict sheepfolds across Cumbria into a scattered set of linked sculptures, working with master dry-stone wallers to make a range of interventions in the structures and their placement in the landscape.[6] A celebration of vernacular architecture and local construction techniques, *Sheepfolds* is also a monument to the labour of forgotten farmers and shepherds: made obsolete by enclosure, by consolidation of flocks on larger farms and by technological advances, the old stone structures are relics of a time when the high fells were grazed as common land. Alongside these social and

An ancient rowan, mossy and lichenous, shades the track to Hallaig, Raasay.

Ruins of a house at Hallaig, Raasay. Rowans now people the crags above the village.

historical aspects, the work engages, too, with how culture is enfolded in longer timescales and larger elemental forces. Where an old drove route passes through a glaciated valley, Goldsworthy placed huge erratic boulders in a series of linked folds, drawing attention to the congruence of human movement with deeper patterns of geology and climate and implying an analogy between the ephemeral physical energies of sheep and the slower, mostly imperceptible motions of stone.[7]

At Mountjoy Farm near Kendal, Goldsworthy restored folds in the north and south corners of a large, walled field. In each, he placed a massive flat-topped boulder, drilling a hole in which a rowan seedling was planted. Work on the site was begun in December 2000, with Goldsworthy noting that the idea for planting the rowans was inspired by 'a nearby tree . . . seemingly growing out of a stone . . . a powerful example of resilience and strength'.[8] Planting, however, was delayed by an outbreak of foot-and-mouth disease in spring 2001. Many animals were culled, and farming communities struggled to weather the financial and emotional loss. Such dramatic circumstances only

Andy Goldsworthy, *Young Rowan Just After Planting in the Northern, Mountjoy Tree Folds,*
Underbarrow, Cumbria, December 2001.

intensified the meanings Goldsworthy was already attaching to the
planted rowans, living aspects of the artwork, which he intended
to signify 'the difficulty and precariousness of farming, especially
in upland area' and to evoke 'hardship, struggle, renewal, fragility,
precariousness and strength'.

By completely enclosing the rowans in the folds, which no sheep
can enter, Goldsworthy worked a strange reversal: the trees, previously
thought to offer magical protection to the flocks, are now guarded
from the sheep, which would ordinarily graze on their leaves. Since
completion, at least one of the rowans has withered in the stone. The
leafless tree seems eerily appropriate: each closed fold is a monument to absence, and there is a deathly quality to the museum-like
display of a plant whose meanings no longer live within the context
of seasonal ritual and communal belief.

Goldsworthy has also enlisted rowan in more ephemeral works.
For an early book, he photographed a floating sculpture made on

29 August 1987 from thorn-pinned iris leaves and rowan berries. Bright against the dark surface of the pond – and free to drift across it – this floating form evokes the geometric energies of both Mondrian-esque abstraction and Chinese calligraphy.[9] Like Monet's famous studies of water lilies, it also draws attention to the illusionistic play of depths in the reflective surface. The same season, on 25 October, Goldsworthy laid rowan leaves of various autumnal hues – burgundy, vermilion, ochre, gold – in graded rings around an ink-black hole.[10] Like the sheepfolds, it is a work that explores the allure of circular forms, as well as the idea of a void or nothingness from which the world continually emerges.

Most of all, these leaf and berry works pose questions about colour. For some art historians, the story of modern painting begins

Andy Goldsworthy, *Iris blades pinned together with thorns / filled in five sections with rowan berries / fish attacking from below / difficult to keep all berries in / nibbled by ducks*, Yorkshire Sculpture Park, West Bretton, 29 August 1987.

with the industrial synthesis of pigment.[11] While liberating artists from a long, artisanal training in workshop colour production and allowing them to paint outdoors, this technical achievement also led to a gradual detachment of colour from physical processes and material texture. Unlike the pigments in older artworks, which gain character from the imperfect processing of raw materials and the unpredictable energy of human labour, industrially produced paint is remarkable for its microscopically grained and uniform consistency.[12] Reinvented as a commodity, as clear chromatic units discrete on rainbow charts, colour is available to modern artists as a pure idea: it floats free into a virtual space of playful abstraction.[13]

By working with colours taken directly from nature, colours that cannot be detached from living, irregular bodies, Goldsworthy's art

Andy Goldsworthy, *Rowan leaves laid around a hole / collecting the last few leaves / nearly finished / dog ran into hole / started again / made in the shade on a windy, sunny day*, Yorkshire Sculpture Park, West Bretton, 25 October 1987.

188

expresses a Romantic urge to contest the withdrawal of painting into the self-contained and separate sphere of gallery and canvas. Arranged as they are, and accented by the complementary vivid green of the leaves, his rowan berries assume a revelatory brightness; the familiar is momentarily estranged, challenging assumptions about the division of nature and artifice. 'Fish attacking from below,' Goldsworthy writes, blurbing the iris and rowan work, 'difficult to keep all the berries in/ nibbled at by ducks'.[14] Such works reminds us that, for most of time, colour has been a process and a relation between living entities, not something that can be fixed to a ready-made surface – that our world is so richly pigmented because of plants, the profusion of life they make possible and rely on for their own reproduction.

Finally, there is an undeniably spiritual aspect to Goldsworthy's use of natural materials.[15] Arranged around a dark void, his rowan leaves evoke portals to the spiritual otherworld. Likewise, his sheep-folds draw particular power both from the ancient metaphorical association of the flock with the Church, and through reference to the circular forms of ancient monuments. In the Mountjoy Folds, the stone boulders planted with rowans are reminiscent of altars, the shed berries of sacrificial blood.

Such works create pathos through a nostalgic celebration of lost forms of ritual community – a congregation implicitly rooted in landscape and in proximity to nature rather than in any particular religious system. In this respect, Goldsworthy participates in a trad-ition of twentieth-century art and writing that has sought to engage with the impact of disenchantment and existential uprooting, both personal and communal, by imagining or discovering ancient forms of nature worship. Given its longstanding reputation as a powerfully enchanted species, especially in Celtic societies, it is hardly surprising that rowan has played a prominent role in such a tradition.

Especially influential in this regard is the work of the poet, novel-ist and classicist Robert Graves. In the 1940s, Graves began work on what would become *The White Goddess* – a bewildering melange of literary history, comparative mythology, religious anthropology and

Celtic revivalism. First published in 1948, and reissued in revised editions in 1952 and 1961, *The White Goddess* achieved a surprise best-seller status, enjoying an enormous influence on twentieth-century occultism, neo-paganism and New Age spirituality.[16] The book's central argument is that Welsh and Irish literature of the early medieval period is cryptically animated by the arcane knowledge of an ancient matriarchal religion and its ritual year – a spiritual wisdom once guarded by Druids and bards and written down in the mysterious ogham alphabet.[17] It is a conclusion reached through a range of highly eccentric hermeneutic methods, most since contested by more conventional scholarship.

The rowan plays a significant role in Graves's fanciful reconstruction of archaic religion. It appears in his description of the titular goddess – 'deathly pale face, lips red as rowan-berries, startlingly blue eyes'– and is associated with the second lunar month in a calendar of 'seasonal tree magic'.[18] In this latter guise, rowan presides over the important Celtic feast of Imbolc, a celebration of the returning sunshine and the first stirrings of spring. Graves associates it with St Brigit, who he sees as a Christian proxy for a conjectured Celtic fire goddess, Brigid, herself a manifestation of the 'White Goddess, the quickening Triple Muse'.[19]

Drawing on the medieval Irish text *Auraicept na n-Éces* (The Scholar's Primer), Graves also connects the rowan with the second letter (*Luis*) of the early Irish ogham alphabet, a script used mainly in Ireland from the first to sixth centuries and now found primarily on ceremonial stones believed to indicate land ownership. Likely begun in the seventh century, but expanded and revised into the twelfth, the *Auraicept* is a mythic reconstruction of the history of the Irish vernacular, tracing it back to the biblical Tower of Babel. In the process, the text provides an important origin for the still-influential idea that each ogham letter was derived from a particular tree, using etymological kennings called 'word ogham' to link each letter to a different species. According to the *Auraicept*, the name *Luis* derives from the phrase *lí súla*, 'delight of the eye', a meaning that connects it with the rowan 'owing to the beauty of [the rowan's] berries'.[20] Though most scholars now discount the idea that ogham letter-names derived from trees, this does offer a compelling insight into the longstanding aesthetic appreciation of rowan.

For Graves, the destruction and displacement of ancient Celtic tradition by Christianity was the culmination of a universal historical pattern: the once-widespread worship of a mother goddess, personification of fertile nature, violently ousted by patriarchal, proto-rationalist rites. While the old religion preached fear and veneration of the natural world, its profanation precipitated a spiritual history of disenchantment and desecration. Humanity, Graves laments, has 'turned the house upside down by capricious experiments in philosophy, science and industry', creating

> a civilization in which the prime emblems of poetry are dishonoured. In which serpent, lion and eagle belong to the circus-tent; ox, salmon and boar to the cannery; racehorse and greyhound to the betting ring; and the sacred grove to the sawmill.[21]

Graves's stirring denunciations of the military-industrial complex and the allure of the arcane knowledge he claimed to have revived would strike a chord with the anti-capitalist counterculture of the 1960s. He entered correspondence with a range of religionists, including a leading figure in the modern Wiccan movement, Gerald Gardner. Many ideas first made accessible by Graves – that rowan is sacred to the fire goddess Brigid, for example – are now routinely quoted as facts about ancient Celtic spirituality in the burgeoning sphere of Internet arcana. Being so well known, Graves's motifs are also ripe for parody. In Seamus Heaney's short lyric 'Song', for example, Graves's rowan-lipped goddess is subject to a subtle deflation and reversal, as the speaker notes 'a rowan like a lipsticked girl'.[22]

Committed, like Graves, to an ideal of spiritual wisdom still glimpsed in the inspiration of poets, few artists have placed the rowan

tree so squarely at the centre of their life and writing as the poet and
scholar Kathleen Raine.[23] Raine's mother's ancestry was Scottish and,
growing up in suburban Essex, the young poet saw her displacement
from a fantasized Gaelic motherland as characteristic of a spiritual
exile – both historical and metaphysical. Indeed, in her autobiographical writings and poetry, Raine figures the alienation of Celtic
tradition within a modern, anglicized Britain as a social analogue

Sapling rowans growing in the woods above Sandaig Bay. The place became
an archetype of Eden for Kathleen Raine, the rowan its Tree of Life.

for each individual soul's forgetting of its origin in the divine – a
recapitulation of the Fall. Celtic Scotland, in other words, became,
for Raine, a kind of gateway to the lost Eden.[24]

This mythic sense of Scotland as a privileged spiritual terrain was
a key ingredient in Raine's ill-fated infatuation with the aristocratic
writer and naturalist Gavin Maxwell. Introduced by Raine's publisher,

the pair met in London in 1949.[25] Maxwell, of course, would later be made famous by the success of *Ring of Bright Water*, his account of living with otters in a remote West Highland cottage at Sandaig. (He called it Camusfeàrna, 'Bay of the Alders'.) 'I had met by miracle another person who came from my first world,' Raine writes in her memoir, *The Lion's Mouth*, 'and because he came from the places where Eden had been, it was as if he came from Eden itself.'[26]

Soon after this first meeting, Raine recorded a vision that affirmed her sense that Maxwell would play a special role in her spiritual life. Late one night, she found herself suddenly able to see 'into two worlds, as if, waking, one were at the same time to explore a dream'. At the centre of the hallucination was a rowan with 'its clusters of white flowers'. At the foot of the tree, a boy of twelve or so was sleeping. Raine perceived that the rowan was his dream and that he was dreaming a vision of life flowing through the tree — waters rising to its roots and into its trunk and branches, leaf and flower unfurling, a blackbird singing from the green shade of the foliage. The dream, she felt certain, was 'an anamnesis of the soul's native place', the dreamer, Gavin, a facet of her own immortal spirit. 'I saw neither serpent nor wall . . . my tree stood wild and free': this visionary rowan was Raine's own Tree of Life, a symbol of the power of creative imagination to reunite her with the divine sources of being.[27]

The vision was written up into a poem, the fifth in Raine's *Northumbrian Sequence* and an archetypal statement of her ideal of the inspired poet as 'the sleeper at the rowan's foot'.[28] She presented it to Maxwell only to find that he, too, had written a poem incorporating a mystic vision of the rowan. For Raine, this was deepest confirmation of their spiritual connection: 'as if one consciousness lived us both . . . we evoked, each in the other, the archetype of Eden . . . the Tree of Life.'[29]

It is difficult, from Raine's version of events — so heavily freighted, in every detail, with personal–mythical significance — to develop a realistic sense of the relationship between the pair. It was an intense yet sexless arrangement. Maxwell, though later married, was homosexual, allowing Raine to share his bed only once — and on condition that they did not touch. She likely tolerated this physical distance since it affirmed the spiritual aura of the bond. Certainly, it seems unlikely that Maxwell experienced the same cultish feeling about their connection as Raine did. She is tellingly unmentioned in his *Ring of Bright Water*. Instead, he was in the strange position of finding his real origins – Scottish, aristocratic – coinciding with Raine's most powerful fantasies, fantasies that had as much to do with intense snobbery and class insecurity as with her fervent religiosity and powerful sense of poetic vocation.

What we do know is that Raine helped Maxwell with his literary career. In return, he lent her the house at Sandaig where she cared for his otter, Mijbil, while he was away. At Sandaig, Raine found her Eden made real: 'I first saw that house in the early-evening, the sun pouring gold across the sea from beyond Skye . . . and the rowan-tree before the house.'[30] The wild landscapes of the place inspired a poetry of celebration and lament in which the rowan offers a now-familiar access to occult enlightenment. 'The Wilderness', from Raine's 1965 collection, *The Hollow Hill*, is typical in this regard.[31] The poem opens with a sense of regret: the poet has arrived in this world too late; old gods have vanished from the land, their magic and lore forsaken; an ancient culture has gone. And yet, in place of shared language and ritual, Raine finds that something still remains. The landscape needs a poet to read and revive its magic words, to recognize the form 'of Eden where the lonely rowan bends over the dark pool'. If the rowan is Raine's tree of knowledge, then it is the poet's gamble to have 'tasted the bitter berries red'.[32]

Bitterness, not wisdom, would be the lasting flavour of the tale. One summer, Gavin came to Sandaig with a lover. He expected Kathleen to leave the house, to stay at the cottage of a nearby friend. The insult brought slowly surfacing resentments and insecurities to a head. 'I left the house', she wrote, 'in all the anguish of my real or imagined rejection, and went to the rowan-tree . . . Weeping I laid my hands on the trunk, calling upon the tree for justice: "Let Gavin suffer, in this place, as I am suffering now."'[33]

Memorial stone to Gavin Maxwell at the site of his cottage on Sandaig Bay, Knoydart,
Scotland. In her autobiography, Raine states that 'she laid in his grave a bunch of
rowan-berries from the Tree'.

Striking at the very centre of their bond, she had evoked a tradition
of magical belief – in the rowan as a tree of special power, in the efficacy of words – which was also central to her self-identity as a poet.
Whether for her belief in the direct effect of the curse, or for what she
felt it revealed about the darkness of her deepest nature, Raine would
later hold herself responsible for Maxwell's subsequent misfortune:
for the loss of Mijbil and the destruction by fire of the house at
Sandaig, for Maxwell's own premature death from cancer in 1969.

Maxwell himself became aware of Raine's imprecation by reading a draft of *The Lion's Mouth*. In the third volume of his memoirs
of Camusfeàrna, *Raven Seek Thy Brother*, he saw the value of the story
as a source of lurid fascination, making it central to an autobiographical narrative of disillusionment and loss. After Maxwell's early
death, Raine's feelings of remorse and despair intensified. Finally, in
1976, she published the long poem *On a Deserted Shore*, a cathartic
elegy for their relationship. The poem's final words, addressed directly
to Maxwell, poignantly exploit the rich ambiguity of Raine's rowan
and its personal symbolism: '*Shall you and I, in all the journeyings of soul,/
Remember the rowan tree, the waterfall?*'[34] It is an image that counterposes

the thin, religious dream of an abstract heaven – the 'journeyings of soul' beyond death – with an altogether earthier and more potent longing: return to Sandaig, the rowan. Despite her spirituality, Raine seems to admit that, often, paradise will have been the very place we are: it is a shape of sensation, an unfurling of memory seeded by something deep in the piquancy of feeling.

Despite her elitism, Raine's idealism often discloses a longing rooted in universally accessible sensations. It is a quality that brings her closer to the spirit of Pasternak and Tsvetaeva – *Bright, bitter berries / from the rowan tree*. For all these writers, the rowan, its clustered berries, bitter and beautiful, is a living reminder of the world's profound strangeness and excess, its uncanny otherworldliness. Heaven, these writers tell us, is not elsewhere. Just look again at the rowan, its autumn gleam.

The Survivor rowan in a recent photograph. The small seedlings on the bank are the tree's offspring, able to flourish in the absence of sheep.

Conclusion
Where One Tree Survives

In 2021, a 'quite ordinary' rowan tree, no more than a century old, was the UK's entry for 'European Tree of the Year'.[1] Already chosen as Scotland's favourite tree of 2020, 'The Survivor' was entered for the prize by members of the Borders Forest Trust (BFT), a grassroots conservation charity working in the country's southern uplands.

The Survivor grows in the Carrifran valley, a craggy, glaciated glen ascending to the peaty raised plateau at the heart of the Moffat and Tweedsmuir hills. Head northeast from Moffat on the A708 towards Selkirk and you climb the cradling sweep of Moffatdale. Following the river, Moffat Water, the road steadily ascends along its ancient route into a dramatic landscape shaped by sporadic invasions of Pleistocene ice. Carrifran is one of a sequence of side valleys abutting the north flank of the main glen. Roughly parallel to one another, they are separated by high wind-swept saddles of heathered greywacke.

In the last glacial period – until as recently as 14,000 years ago – these subsidiary valleys held deep glaciers, each heaving down to a larger ice sheet in the central dale.[2] Today, each is a distinct watershed, with Carrifran nursing its braided burn through an area of over 6 sq. km (2 sq. mi.). It is above this river, on a steep tussocky bank, that The Survivor rowan stands. Rising to the impressive symmetrically fanned crown of a nursery specimen, its natural tilted beginnings are nevertheless evident in the taut, bow-like arc of its smooth trunk.

The Survivor rowan in a treeless Carrifran valley, 1990s.

After two years of fundraising, the BFT completed the purchase of Carrifran from a local landowner at the turn of the millennium. In taking ownership of the valley, the trust was able to begin the realization of a dream it had conceived years earlier:

> To re-create in the Southern Uplands an extensive tract of mainly forested wilderness, with most of the rich diversity of native species that was present in the area before human activities became dominant ... Access will be open to all, and we hope that it will be used throughout the next millennium as an inspirational and educational resource.[3]

On 1 January 2000, more than one hundred people gathered at Carrifran to plant the first new seedlings in the partially frozen earth.

A treeless Carrifran in 1989, before the work of ecological restoration began.

When members of the BFT had first visited the site in summer 1996, Carrifran, like most upland landscapes in modern Britain, was almost entirely devoid of trees. Right up to the high cusp of the watershed, sheep, feral goats and deer had browsed down all but the most crag-protected specimens. Indeed, so overstocked was the land that even heather had begun to retreat, replaced by a khaki desert of rough grasses and tumbledown scree. Only the presence of The Survivor hinted at the valley's woodland past.

The region's accelerating deforestation by sheep can be traced back to the Middle Ages, when monasteries entered the international wool trade. With the Scottish Clearances of the eighteenth and nineteenth centuries, grazing of smaller flocks on upland commons gave way to extensive sheepwalks and booming stock numbers.[4] Finally, in the twentieth century, the process intensified still further, as technological

advances and agricultural subsidies based on 'headage' and an obligation to remove 'unwanted vegetation on agricultural land', practically
guaranteed overgrazing.[5] So widespread is this pattern in Britain that,
for many, wilderness has come to be primarily associated with such
dun, wind-blasted vistas. Standing at the centre of this slow devastation of place – safe, somehow, in its riparian fastness – The Survivor
was quickly adopted by the BFT as a symbol of ecological possibility.
'Where one tree survives . . . a million trees will grow' – thus announced
the charity's fundraising leaflets from the time, a hopeful slogan
accompanied by an emblematic photo of the solitary rowan.[6]

As it raised funds for the realization of this dream, the BFT also
sought wider expertise in how to proceed in an ecologically sensitive
manner. Many Scottish hillsides have been afforested for commercial
purposes in the past half-century. Most, however, are planted with
geometric arrangements of non-native conifers – like the larches
that so offended Dorothy Wordsworth at the Falls of Bruar. Aside
from the trees themselves, such plantation monocultures are often
devoid of ecological richness, lacking the complex soil biology, diverse
ground flora and dynamic trophic interactions of mature mixed
woodland. Whereas planted larch and fir are each associated with
less than twenty invertebrate species, an oak or willow in old woods
can support close to three hundred different insects.[7] At Dundreggan,
a restoration project in the Scottish Highlands run by Trees for Life,
Alan Watson Featherstone, the charity's founder, has documented
the extraordinary biological richness associated with a single rowan
in mature woodland.[8] Dubbed 'The Wonder Tree', Featherstone's
rowan was home to a specialist aphid, *Dysaphis sorbi*, which tapped the
tree for sap. A colony of rare wood ants, *Formica lugubris*, sustained itself
by milking honeydew from the aphids. Also feeding on the spilt sugars
were wasps and hoverflies, while tree slugs and orb-weaver spiders
thrived along the bark and among the branches. On the undersides
of leaves, Featherstone found tiny mite galls and the fragile egg casings
of moths. In a flourishing ecosystem, the rowan can be a framework
for many linked and overlapping worlds.

·CARRIFRAN·
WILDWOOD

Where one tree survives ....

Founders bought the valley -
Stewards can help restore it!

Ecological restoration in the Southern Uplands of Scotland
BORDERS FOREST TRUST in association with the JOHN MUIR TRUST
The Wildwood Website: www.carrifran.org.uk

The Survivor rowan as pictured on an original fundraising leaflet made by the
Wildwood Group, Borders Forest Trust.

Unlike commercial foresters, and inspired by initiatives such as
Trees for Life, the BFT's goal was never simply to plant trees. They
set out, instead, to seed rich and functioning ecosystems, matching
them to the soil, geology and climate of the region. Doing so, they
hoped, would stimulate environmental processes that could become

self-sustaining, drawing biodiversity back to the valley and initiating a complex cascade of interactions between species at all levels of the food-chain. As the purchase of Carrifran neared completion, the BFT set out to design a management plan that would bring these ideas to life.

As luck would have it, the charity was able to access a rich set of data on the woodland history of the valley. A few years previously, the site had provided evidence for one of the most detailed analyses of historical pollen deposits in any upland area in the UK. In 1990, a broken yew-wood bow, the oldest known in Britain, was found in peat bogs skirting the northern rim of Carrifran – an area of sumped and claggy ground between ridges called Rotten Bottom. Carbon dating showed it had been left there some 6,000 years previously by a Mesolithic hunter.[9] Likely part of a nomadic clan migrating up Moffatdale to fish, this prehistoric archer was also a competitor with bears, wolves and lynx for the region's abundant wild game: auroch, elk, boar and red deer.[10] Because of the archaeological importance of this find, the National Trust for Scotland had sought sponsors to carry out an analysis of peat at the site, excavating long-buried evidence of the landscape the hunter had moved through.

Peat began to form at Rotten Bottom over 10,000 years ago, after the final retreat of the glaciers. Peat soil results when water inhibits microbial decomposition, leading to a seasonal build-up of dead plant material. Vegetation is laid down in strata, like Arctic ice or the radial accumulation of tree rings. In the process, grains of atmospheric pollen are captured at the surface and then sealed over by successive layers, so that a trench dug into peat is a wondrous palaeoecological time machine. Using radiocarbon dating to reveal the age of each stratum, a precise linear chronology can be defined; microscopic analysis of the pollen present in each layer then creates a picture of changing ecological conditions through time.

Written into the lower reaches of the Rotten Bottom peat was the signature of a region slowly reforested after ice withdrew.[11] Analysis revealed that birches came first, with hazel shortly after; juniper and pine were followed closely by elm, oak and ash. Though its pollen is hard to detect, it is likely that rowan, a pioneer species quickly spread by migrant birds, was also among these earliest returning trees. By the time the hunter stood at the quaking edge of the bog, disposing of the broken bow, the valley below may have reached a peak of woodland diversity.[12] Oak, ash, alder, birch and elm were growing there with rowan, hawthorn, aspen, hazel and holly. Various cherries were present; willows, too, especially in sparse montane woodland on the upper slopes.

Living as they did in a landscape of woods and scrubby clearings, it is likely these Mesolithic peoples possessed a vibrant mythological and religious repertoire, with trees playing a prominent spiritual role in their communal lives.[13] Might the deposition of the bow have been an offering to the local gods of this numinous upland place? Perhaps the archer sought out the valley's red rowans as sites for ritual activity or for the gathering of talismanic material. Whatever the exact purpose of their journey, the Mesolithic archer of Rotten Bottom looked out on woodlands that were reaching a post-glacial climax state, a place brimming with interconnected life. This long-lost vision, buried in the peat, would offer an imaginative benchmark for the BFT's management plan at Carrifran.

With the pollen analysis from Rotten Bottom giving a fine-grained history of the valley's vanished woods, the next step was to match this historic ecology to present woodland communities on similar sites. As millennium day drew closer, a scientific assessment of all aspects of Carrifran's climate, soil and hydrology was initiated, helping to map out areas suitable for distinct woodland types as defined by the National Vegetation Classification. Such detailed planning gave a precise sense of the relative frequency of different species to be planted out in each zone, allowing time for seed to be gathered from relict woodlands in the area, and for the first seedlings to be established.

Loosely, it was decided that much of the valley, especially at lower altitudes, would be defined by upland woods composed mainly of sessile oak and downy birch. These woods would also support holly, aspen, hazel, elm, willow, bird cherry, hawthorn, juniper and rowan in varying proportions. Rowan would account for about 20 per cent of the planting in these zones. At higher altitudes, and in various niches created by steeper slopes, it would also be possible to create rare examples of montane scrub and treeline juniper woodland, both also supporting small wind-suppressed rowans.[14]

As the arboreal mascot for this intensely researched, intricately imagined scheme, The Survivor represents so much more than the numerical promise of its accompanying slogan. It is a representative of the desire to allow a truly *living* landscape to return to the southern uplands. With the help of volunteers, the BFT has now overseen the strategic planting of more than 750,000 trees in the valley. Sheep and feral goats have been excluded by a perimeter fence, and deer are culled annually in low numbers. Before long, The Survivor will disappear from easy view, blurring into a dense woodland dotted with

A more recent view up the valley showing regenerating woodlands with rowan, birch and sessile oak.

its own offspring. Already, rowans are the first trees in the valley that have begun to spread naturally. Older specimens are surrounded by dense thickets of suckering subsidiary trunks – exploratory clones that were previously coppiced off by browsing ruminant mouths. Their roots are drawing up minerals and nutrients long missing from the depleted soil; their falling leaves, twigs and berries will rot down, making new earth for new trees. These pioneer rowans are fulfilling a hope represented by The Survivor: landscapes restored to the base-line ecological richness at which dynamic processes of transformation and growth will carry on unaided.[15]

The Survivor rowan, then, is a symbol whose meaning transcends the presence of trees at Carrifran. It is a threshold messenger for bot-anical life of all kinds: for the wild honeysuckle that now trails its scented whorls among the branches; for the dark luxuriant ivy sprawl-ing across wet streamside rocks and onto young trunks; for bluebells and wood anemone beneath the oaks; for scarce mountain flowers now spreading on higher slopes – mossy saxifrage, mountain sorrel, bog bilberry and roseroot.[16] It is also a herald for the arrival of birds. Bird surveys at Carrifran, carried out in comparative parallel with those for the neighbouring, still-deforested valley of Black Hope, provide some of the first and most comprehensive data on the return of bird life to newly planted broad-leaf woodland in the UK. Since the millennium, nineteen new species have been recorded as summer residents at Carrifran. Many hundreds of breeding willow warblers are joined by blackcap and lesser redpoll; by dunnock, garden warbler and siskin; by mistle thrush, tree pipit, woodcock and song thrush; by wood warbler and tawny owl. Jays are now in the valley, lending their brute beaks to planting efforts by burying the first new acorns in the soil. Troops of blue and great tit flit among the leaves, guzzling invertebrates that flourish in the oak and birch. In winter, fieldfare, redwing and blackbirds are regular visitors, harvesting the berry crop from Carrifran's rowans. Above them all are buzzards, peregrine fal-cons and the occasional golden eagle – magnificent gifts of all the riotous solar energy captured by the planted woods.[17]

The Survivor with its self-seeded offspring.

In the years since its initial purchase of land, the BFT has been able to buy further sites across the Moffat and Tweedsmuir hill. Its long-term goal is the creation of linked areas of wild habitat, a 'Wild Heart of Southern Scotland' restoring parts of the ancient Ettrick Forest. Large-scale restoration of wild land would make it possible to return species such as lynx, boar and beaver to the area. Charismatic mammals such as these – of which Britain has lost more than almost any other European nation – play an essential role in allowing wild ecosystems to flourish.[18] With lynx returning, for example, there would be less need to cull deer in the Carrifran valley. Beavers would fell trees, leaving dead wood – home to a huge variety of insects, bryophytes and fungi – and creating disturbed areas for wildflowers and specialist wetland plants to flourish.[19] Rootling in the earth for buried acorns and grubs, boars would disturb the soil, giving light, windblown

Another old rowan at Carrifran, which, in the absence of grazing, has put forth a prodigious growth of new shoots.

seed an opportunity to germinate. In the absence of boar, the trust now plans to graze pigs in the summer valley: suppressing bracken and dense grass, they will accelerate the natural regeneration of trees.[20]

More than anything, then, The Survivor is a symbol of interconnected life, of the kaleidoscopic interactions of species – from top predators to microscopic mycelium – in any developed ecosystem. From this perspective, it is most appropriate that the tree should be a rowan. As a magnet for migrating birds, the tree's berries are a prominent and easily visible focus for ecologies that transcend the local. But as well as alerting us to the vital connectedness of space, the rowan is also a marker of time. In his 1977 poem 'Rowan berry', the Scottish poet Norman MacCaig humorously ventriloquizes an individual berry on the tree. MacCaig's berry speaks with the self-importance and optimism of youth: recognizing itself as one of many, it nevertheless believes its own destiny to be paramount and central. The berry knows that, along with most of its 'cousins', it will be eaten by birds, that its seed will be 'dropped' arbitrarily. And yet it celebrates this devastation as the means of its posterity, eagerly anticipating its future as a mature plant 'swaying and swinging' with its own 'genealogy of berries'.[21] Despite its light-heartedness, MacCaig's poem captures an essential connection between time's unfolding and the incorrigible plurality of the natural world. A berry, properly considered, rewilds the present. Each moment, it tells us, is a thicket of possibility, a branching path defined by the concatenating interactions of the now.

By the time MacCaig wrote his poem, the berry's breezy confidence of reproductive success was surely misplaced. Since the Industrial Revolution, it is the human *now* – the sped-up present of market and money – which dominates our earthly time. In the Anthropocene epoch, human presence is so total as to be etched into the solid geology of tomorrow – in plastiglomerate rocks and traces of nuclear fallout, in technofossils and the carbonaceous particles deposited by burning fossil fuels.[22] Since the Romantic period, the rowan, as a symbol, has tracked this tilting balance of nature and culture. So often, as we've seen in previous chapters, the tree has been made a marker of lost and displaced possibilities – of alternative states of relation between nature and the human. Though often utopian or nostalgic, such visions have always been based on an attempt to see the natural world as something other than a quantifiable resource. They constitute a record of authentic desires and needs beyond the calculus of growth and profit.

When first adopted as an emblem by the BFT, The Survivor stood out as an eloquent summation of this history. In its drastic isolation, the tree spoke powerfully of an era of biodiversity loss and habitat destruction. In England, more native woodland was destroyed in the thirty years after the Second World War than in the previous three centuries.[23] In a similar timeframe, Britain lost over 97 per cent of its traditionally managed, species-rich grasslands and an estimated 44 million breeding birds.[24] In 2019, the *State of Nature* report discovered that 41 per cent of over 8,000 plant and animal species surveyed had declined in the past half-century, and 133 species vanished entirely from the UK during the same period; around 15 per cent of species are currently threatened with extinction in the archipelago.[25]

Though notably extreme, the British picture is a microcosm of global loss. As climate change accelerates, we find ourselves at an historical juncture in which MacCaig's sense of time as fertile with potential repercussion obtains a terrifying existential weight. In a connected world, our individual actions – buying groceries, driving to work, upgrading a phone – assume a cumulative resonance whose consequences often exceed our understanding and control. At Carrifran, and places like it, an attempt is being made to counteract this grim picture. More than a marker of loss or focus for nostalgia, The Survivor reclaims a positive, active dimension for the symbolism of rowan. It is an emblem of regeneration and the power of local movements to enact meaningful change, creating new and enriched human connections in the process.

As part of mature, mixed woodlands, especially in the uplands, rowans capture carbon, lessen the flood impact of rain and boost biodiversity. Making spaces for contemplation, a shelter from the frantic attentional demands of a networked society, rowans offer experiences of beauty and a sense of intimacy with non-human life.[26] More than anything, grassroots investment in local ecology enables forms of solidarity based on bioregional, rather than national or ethnic identifications: it grows community – potentially as porous, connected and diverse as the ecosystem itself – from the ground up.[27] The Survivor, like many rowans past, is a gateway to long-suppressed otherworlds.

Across the hills from Carrifran – 65 km (40 mi.) or so, as the eagle flies – sits Little Sparta, the garden created by the poet, artist and publisher Ian Hamilton Finlay. Like Carrifran, Little Sparta is an enclave, a provocation and the statement of an alternative present. But where the former is energized by a vision of Mesolithic woods and the latest ecological science, Finlay's garden world is a product of the eclectic obsessions of its creator: pre-Socratic philosophy and classical myth; boats and the lexicon of sea-fishing; the Second World War armaments; the history of Western landscape art; the militant commitment and aphoristic force of the French revolutionary Louis de Saint-Just.[28] 'Certain gardens are described as retreats,' Finlay wrote, in one of his 'Detached Sentences on Gardening', 'when they are really attacks.'[29] It is a statement that captures Finlay's vision quite beautifully, and with characteristic wit. Though apparently a place of retirement, Little Sparta was envisioned by its maker as an assault on prevailing values. A haven of creative intellect and transformative contemplation, the garden also unsettles and confronts.[30] It is a place of ideas and of spare, imbricated poetry.

In the woodland garden, an upright rectangular stone beneath a young rowan bears an italicized inscription:

The Rowan
Is Learning
To Write

In direct light, the rowan sapling casts its shadow on the stone, marking time in an asemic script of leaf and berry, twig and bud, corymb and perching bird. A parallel is implied between language and the unfolding of natural processes – I'm reminded of the idea that ogham letters took their names from trees.

Most of all, what I like about this installation is that it asks us to consider the tree as an active participant in the creation of meaning, rather than the passive recipient of our projections. In front of Finlay's sculpture, or in a place like Carrifran, we have a chance to pause and attend, letting new ecologies of mind take shape. We are reminded that to destroy and diminish the natural world is also to erase our own potential thoughts and ideas: the bright and multiple thought of

Robin Gillanders, *The Rowan Is Learning to Write*, 1997, silver gelatin print, the garden of the sculptor Ian Hamilton Finlay.

sudden berries on a grey winter street; the luminous, feathery thought of layered leaves, light held in their susurrating verdancy; the stark, italic thought of trunk and branch, pale against the looming granite of a crag.[31]

Timeline

54–36 million years ago (Eocene epoch)	Evolution of broad-leaved deciduous trees. Possible appearance of first ancestral rowans
2 million–15,000 years ago (Pleistocene epoch)	*Sorbus aucuparia* disperses throughout Europe during interglacial periods
32,000 BCE	'Red Lady' buried in Haviland Cave, Wales. Indication of the early sacramental importance of the colour red in northern Europe
10,000 years ago (early Holocene epoch)	*Sorbus aucuparia* joins trees such as birch, willow, alder, aspen, oak and pine in woodlands returning to northern Europe after glaciation
6,000 years ago	Rowan berries form part of the diet of Mesolithic settlers in southern Sweden – and likely across northern Europe
7th century	Earliest date for the Irish vernacular treatise *Auraicept na n-Éces* (The Scholar's Primer), which invents tree names for each letter of the ogham alphabet. Rowan is associated with the second letter, *Luis*, a connection explained by a fanciful etymology from *lí súla*, meaning 'delight of the eye' – evidence of a longstanding aesthetic appreciation of the tree
9th century	Vikings establish permanent settlements in Ireland – some scholars see the magical importance of rowan in Ireland as derived from Scandinavian influence. *Bald's Leechbook*, an Anglo-Saxon medical compendium, advises the use of *cwic-beam* (a tree name that likely refers to rowan) bark in healing poultices

10th century	*Þórsdrápa* (Poem about Thor) composed by Eilífr Goðrúnarson during a time of religious and political upheaval in the Scandinavian world. The poem provides the earliest evidence of the myth of Thor's crossing of the River Vimur, in which a rowan bush saves the god from drowning. In the thirteenth century, Snorri Sturluson, in *Edda*, presented this myth as the origin of the apparently idiomatic phrase 'Thor's salvation is a rowan'
11th century	Manuscript of West Saxon 'field blessing' charm, *Æcerbot*, which makes use of crosses of *cwic-beam*
12th–15th centuries	Compilation of the great codices of early Irish literature, most written in monastic settings. These manuscripts, such as *The Book of the Dun Cow* (1106), *The Book of Leinster* (1150 and after) and *The Book of Ballymote* (c. 1390), contain surviving texts of a written corpus that linguistic evidence suggests began to take shape around the turn of the eighth century, and which was likely based on even earlier oral material. Tales such as *The Cattle Raid of Fróech*, *The Wooing of Étaín*, *The Siege of Knocklong* and *Cormac's Adventure in the Land of Promise* contain references to rowan that give tantalizing hints to its place in archaic religious beliefs and evidence of Christian writers' reworkings of native pagan lore
16th century	In the 1550s, Mikael Agricola records pagan customs in Finland, including a rare reference to 'Rauni', a goddess possibly associated with the rowan tree as wife of the northern thunder god, Ukko. In his *Daemonologie* (1597), King James VI of Scotland (later James I of England) condemns 'dafte wives' who attach 'roun-trees to the haire or tailes' of livestock. Isobell Watsonne, accused of witchcraft, admits to healing worms with a rowan-wood charm (1590s)
17th century	In *Sylva* (1664), John Evelyn notes the usefulness of rowan wood for tool handles and bows, as well as the use of its berries for flavouring drinks. Geoffrey Keating, in *History of Ireland* (c. 1634), mentions that rowan is known in Ireland as *fid na ndruad* – the Druid's tree. Russian peasants are recorded passing infants through the branches of a rowan decorated with icons to St Paraskeva, a ritual of healing. Testimony from witchcraft

trials includes evidence of the use of rowan by 'cunning' men and women

18th century	In his *Flora Scotica* (1777), John Lightfoot records numerous magical uses of rowan in Scotland, as well as the tree's frequent presence around 'Druidic circles of stone'. Capability Brown plants over 15,000 rowans and birches in the parks and woods at Chatsworth, Derbyshire. William Gilpin remarks on the beauty of rowan when properly 'blended' into picturesque landscape
1800–1850	Samuel Taylor Coleridge features a rowan in his poem 'The Picture; or, The Lover's Resolution' (1802), while William Wordsworth celebrates the tree's beauty in *The Excursion* (1814). Dorothy and William Wordsworth plant rowans in the gardens of Dove Cottage and Rydal Mount. *The Scotish Minstrel* (1822), a collection of 'national song', includes 'The Rowan Tree' by Carolina Oliphant, Lady Nairne. Elias Lönnrot gathers oral poetry in rural Finland, compiling it into the epic *Kalevala* (1849): the rowan makes frequent appearances as a sacred and magical tree, also being associated with patriarchal notions of idealized femininity
1850–75	German chemist A. W. von Hofmann isolates sorbic acid from rowan berries (1859); it will later be patented for use as a preservative and synthesized via an industrial process. John Everett Millais's portrait of the art critic John Ruskin contains the first recognizable rowan in a major British painting
1875–1900	Canon J. C. Atkinson donates rowan amulets gathered from his Yorkshire parish of Danby to the Pitt Rivers Museum, Oxford (1892). William Butler Yeats has a vision of fairies carrying rowan berries on the Sligo coast and writes 'The Danaan Quicken Tree' (1893). He and George Russell develop the nationalistic 'Order of Celtic Mysteries' (1890s), in which the rowan tree has a prominent place as a focus for Celtic magic and mysticism. Finnish painters such as Akseli Gallen-Kallela, Pekka Halonen and Väinö Blomstedt include rowan in paintings of Finnish nature and myth. Ivan Shishkin paints *Birch and Rowan* (1878)
1900–1925	Celtic Revivalism in Scotland: John Duncan places a rowan branch in the hand of a Celtic divinity in *Riders of the Sidhe* (1911). Russian poet Marina Tsvetaeva makes rowan a personal emblem in her *Poems about Moscow*

1925–50	Irish Folklore Archive creates an extensive record of historic uses of the rowan in rural Ireland, especially around the May Day festival of Beltane and the churning of butter. In 'Homesickness', Marina Tsvetaeva makes rowan the emblem of an 'inner Russia' while in Basil Bunting's 'Ballad of the Morpethshire Farmer', the tree is witness to rural displacement. Robert Graves's *The White Goddess* associates rowan with the second month in an ancient ritual calendar of seasonal tree magic and with a postulated Celtic fire goddess, Brigid. Graves's text, itself a late offshoot of Romantic Celticism, will go on to exercise an enormous influence on the place of rowan in twentieth-century and contemporary occult and New Age religion
1950–75	Boris Pasternak's novel *Doctor Zhivago* (1957) places a rowan at the symbolic heart of its narrative of Russian history and politics. The Gaelic poet Sorley MacLean invokes rowan as a focus for negotiation of displacement and love in 'Hallaig' (1954). The poet and scholar Kathleen Raine makes rowan her talisman of spiritual imagination and later places a curse on Gavin Maxwell while laying her hands on a rowan near his house at Sandaig, Scotland
1975–2000	'The Rowan Is Learning to Write' installed at Ian Hamilton Finlay's garden at Little Sparta. Andy Goldsworthy makes use of rowan berries and leaves in ephemeral site-specific artworks. 'The Survivor' rowan is chosen by the Borders Forest Trust to be an emblem of its ambitions for ecological restoration in southern Scotland
2000–present	Rowans planted in boulders enclosed by sheepfolds at Mountjoy Farm, Cumbria, form part of Andy Goldsworthy's public artwork *Sheepfolds*. Rowans form a major part of the planting at Carrifran valley, an ambitious work of landscape restoration carried out by the Borders Forest Trust, southern Scotland. 'The Survivor' rowan is Scottish 'Tree of the Year' for 2020, and entered into European Tree of the Year 2021

References

Introduction: Thresholds of Nature and Culture

1 Hugh McAllister, *The Genus Sorbus: Mountain Ash and Other Rowans* (Kew, 2005), p. 1.
2 Olivier Raspé, Catherine Findlay and Anne-Laure Jacquemart, 'Biological Flora of the British Isles: *Sorbus aucuparia* L.', *Journal of Ecology*, LXXXVIII/2 (2000), pp. 910–30, p. 910.
3 McAllister, *The Genus Sorbus*, pp. 5–6; Kenneth R. Robertson et al., 'A Synopsis of Genera in Maloideae (Rosaceae)', *Systematic Botany*, XVI/2 (1991).
4 McAllister, *The Genus Sorbus*, p. 16.
5 What follows is largely based on the more detailed account discussed ibid., pp. 15–27.
6 J. A. Fossitt, 'Late Quaternary Vegetation History of the Western Isles of Scotland', *New Phytologist*, CXXXII/1 (1996), pp. 171–96, pp. 189–90.
7 Mats Regnell et al., 'Reconstruction of Environment and History of Use During the Late Mesolithic (Ertebølle Culture) at the Inland Settlement of Bökeberg III, Southern Sweden', *Vegetation History and Archaeobotany*, IV/2 (1995), pp. 78 and 89.
8 Raspé et al., *Sorbus aucuparia*, p. 911.
9 Leif Kullman, 'Temporal and Spatial Aspects of Subalpine Populations of *Sorbus aucuparia* in Sweden', *Annales Botanici Fennici*, XXIII/4 (1986), pp. 267–75, p. 269.
10 Anna Barbati, Piermaria Corona and Marco Marchetti, *European Forest Types: Categories and Types for Sustainable Forest Management Reporting and Policy*, EAA Technical Report, No. 9/2006 (Copenhagen, 2007), p. 36.
11 Raspé et al., *Sorbus aucuparia*, pp. 913–14; J. E. Hall, K. J. Kirby and A. M. Whitbread, *National Vegetation Classification: Field Guide to Woodland* (Peterborough, 2004), pp. 57–9 and 84–8; Alison Averis et al., *An Illustrated Guide to British Upland Vegetation* (Exeter, 2014), pp. 104–6.
12 Barbati et al., *European Forest Types*, pp. 59 and 62–4.
13 McAllister, *The Genus Sorbus*, p. 77.

14 M. O. Hill, D. F. Evans and F. O. Bell, 'Long-Term Effects of Excluding Sheep from Hill Pastures in North Wales', *Journal of Ecology*, LXXX/1 (1992), pp. 1–13, p. 10.

15 Raspé et al., *Sorbus aucuparia*, p. 916.

16 Ibid., pp. 922–3

17 Heikki Tyrväinen, 'The Winter Irruption of the Fieldfare *Turdus pilaris* and the Supply of Rowan-Berries', *Ornis Fennica*, LII (1975), pp. 23–31, p. 23; R. L. Swann, 'Redwings in a Highland Glen', *Scottish Birds*, XII/8 (1983), pp. 260–61; Eric Simms, *British Thrushes* (London, 1978), pp. 109–10.

18 R. K. Cornwallis, 'Four Invasions of Waxwings During 1956–60', *British Birds*, LIV/1 (1961), pp. 1–34.

19 Raymond Duncan, 'The Vagaries of Waxwing Migration', BirdGuides, www.birdguides.com, 9 March 2010.

20 Henning Andersen, 'A Glimpse into the Homeland of the Slavs: Ecological and Cultural Change in Prehistory', *Proceedings of the Seventh UCLA Indo-European Conference, Los Angeles, 1995*, ed. Angela Della Volpe (Washington, DC, 1998), pp. 1–68, p. 11.

21 Fiona Stafford, *The Long, Long Life of Trees* (New Haven, CT, 2016), p. 55.

22 Ibid., and see 'Rowan', Oxford English Dictionary, www.oed.com. For a more comprehensive list of English dialect words, see Geoffrey Grigson, *The Englishman's Flora* (St Albans, 1958), pp. 187–8.

23 Brent Berlin and Paul Kay, *Basic Color Terms: Their Universality and Evolution* (Oxford, 1991), p. 17.

24 Ronald Hutton, *Pagan Britain* (New Haven, CT, 2014), pp. 2–7.

25 Michel Pastoureau, *Red: The History of a Color* (Princeton, NJ, 2017), pp. 16–18; Hutton, *Pagan Britain*, pp. 23–5.

26 Pastoureau, *Red*, pp. 22–9.

27 *Am Faclair Bearg – Scottish Gaelic Dictionary*, www.faclair.com, accessed 15 November 2021.

28 Richard Mabey, *Flora Britannica* (London, 1997), pp. 203–4; Grigson, *Englishman's Flora*, pp. 188–91; Stafford, *Long, Long Life*, pp. 58–61.

29 Grigson, *Englishman's Flora*, p. 191.

30 'Quickbeam', Oxford English Dictionary, www.oed.com.

31 Bruce A. Rosenberg, 'The Meaning of Æcerbot', *Journal of American Folklore*, LXXII/313 (1966), pp. 428–36, p. 429.

32 Ralph Waldo Emerson, 'The Poet', in *Nature and Selected Essays*, ed. Larzer Ziff (London, 2003), p. 271.

33 Roland Barthes, *Mythologies*, trans. Annette Lavers (London, 2000).

34 Tim Robinson, *Stones of Aran: Pilgrimage* (London, 2008), p. 20.

35 John Evelyn, *Silva; or, A Discourse of Forest Trees and the Propagation of Timber in His Majesty's Dominions*, 5th edn (London, 1729), p. 75. For more on rowan-wood tools, see Chris Howkins, *Rowan: Tree of Protection* (Addlestone, 1996), pp. 18–23.

36 Evelyn, *Silva*, p. 75; see Jon E. Lewis, ed., *The Mammoth Book of the Secrets of the SAS and Elite Forces* (London, 2002).

37 Elias Lönnrot, *Kalevala*, trans. Keith Bosley (Oxford, 2008), p. 105.

38 Robert K. Henderson, *The Neighbourhood Forager: A Guide for the Wild Food Gourmet* (Toronto, 2000), p. 68.

39 Alexander N. Shikov et al., 'Medicinal Plants of the Russian Pharmacopoeia; Their History and Applications', *Journal of Ethnopharmacology*, CLIV/3 (2014), pp. 481–536, p. 516.

40 Alexander Yashin, 'A Feast of Rowanberries', in *We the Russians: Voices from Russia*, ed. Colette Shulman (New York, 1972), pp. 118–22, p. 119.

41 Shikov et al., 'Medicinal Plants', p. 516.

42 Ibid.

43 Evelyn, *Silva*, p. 75.

44 Ibid.

45 John Lightfoot, *Flora Scotica; or, A Systematic Arrangement, in the Linnaean Method, of the Native Plants of Scotland and the Hebrides* (London, 1777), vol. I, pp. 256–8.

46 Elizabeth Gaskell, 'The Doom of the Griffiths', in *Lizzie Leigh and Other Tales* (London, 1878), p. 374.

47 Linda V. Thomas, 'PRESERVATIVES: Permitted Preservatives – Sorbic Acid', in *Encyclopedia of Food Microbiology*, ed. Richard K. Robinson (Amsterdam, 1999), pp. 1769–76.

48 For an amazingly comprehensive list, see Patrick Roper, 'Descriptive List of Sorbus Drinks', Rowans, Whitebeams and Service Trees Blog (March 2014), https://rowanswhitebeamsandservicetrees.blogspot.com.

1 Old Gods, New Myths

1 Tomás Ó Cathasaigh, 'Pagan Survivals: The Evidence of Early Irish Narrative', in *Coire Sois, The Cauldron of Knowledge: A Companion to Early Irish Saga*, ed. Matthieu Boyd (Notre Dame, IN, 2014), pp. 35–50; Mark Williams, *Ireland's Immortals: A History of the Gods of Irish Myth* (Princeton, NJ, 2016), pp. 3–5 and 45–9; Christopher Abram, *Myths of the Pagan North: The Gods of the Northmen* (London, 2011), pp. 1–31.

2 Keith Thomas, *Religion and the Decline of Magic* (London, 1991), pp. 29–40; Ronald Hutton, *Pagan Britain* (New Haven, CT, 2013), pp. 335–7.

3 Williams, *Ireland's Immortals*, pp. 195–9.

4 Miranda Aldhouse-Green and Stephen Aldhouse-Green, *The Quest for the Shaman: Shape-Shifters, Sorcerers and Spirit-Healers of Ancient Europe* (London, 2005), p. 186.

5 Eoin MacNeill, trans., *Duanaire Finn: The Book of the Lays of Fionn, Part 1* (London, 1908), pp. 127–30. Available online at https://archive.org.

6 John Carey, 'Time, Space, and the Otherworld', *Proceedings of the Harvard Celtic Colloquium*, VII (1987), pp. 1–27.

7 See, for example, Joseph Falaky Nagy, 'Shamanic Aspects of the "Bruidhean" Tale', *History of Religions*, XX/4 (1981), pp. 302–22.

8 Ibid., p. 306.

9 P. W. Joyce, trans. and ed., *Old Celtic Romances* (London, 1879), p. 190. Available online at www.gutenberg.org.

10 Ibid., p. 191.

11 Ibid., p. 193.
12 Aldhouse-Green, *Quest for the Shaman*, p. 15.
13 Anne Ross, *Pagan Celtic Britain* (London, 1992), p. 85.
14 A. T. Lucas, 'The Sacred Trees of Ireland', *Journal of the Cork Historical and Archaeological Society* LXVIII//207–8 (1963), pp. 46–7.
15 Miranda Aldhouse-Green, *The Celtic Myths: A Guide to the Ancient Gods and Legends* (London, 2015), pp. 126–7; Ross, *Pagan Celtic Britain*, pp. 337–41.
16 Ross, *Pagan Celtic Britain*, p. 340.
17 Tomás Ó Cathasaigh, 'The Pursuit of Diarmaid and Gráinne', in *Coire Sois, The Cauldron of Knowledge*, pp. 466–83.
18 Joyce, *Old Celtic Romances*, p. 314. For *bile*, see Lucas, 'Sacred Trees', and Alden Watson, 'The King, the Poet and the Sacred Tree', *Études Celtiques*, XVIII (1981), pp. 165–80.
19 H. R. Ellis Davidson, *Myths and Symbols in Pagan Europe: Early Scandinavian and Celtic Religions* (New York, 1988), pp. 44–7.
20 Ronald Hutton, *Blood and Mistletoe: The History of the Druids in Britain* (New Haven, CT, 2009), p. 45.
21 Patrick S. Dinneen, ed., *Foras Feasa ar Éirinn: The History of Ireland by Geoffrey Keating D.D.* (London, 1908), vol. II, pp. 349–51. This text and most referenced below are available in full as part of the 'Corpus of Electronic Texts' (CELT), maintained by University College, Cork, https://celt.ucc.ie.
22 Charles Plummer, trans. and ed., *Bethada Náem nÉrenn, Lives of Irish Saints* (Oxford, 1922), vol. II, p. 33. Available online at https://archive.org.
23 Williams, *Ireland's Immortals*, p. 4.
24 Hutton, *Blood and Mistletoe*, pp. 34–44.
25 Sharon Paice MacLeod, *Celtic Cosmology and the Otherworld: Mythic Origins, Sovereignty and Liminality* (Jefferson, NC, 2002), p. 192; Alberto Ferreiro, *Simon Magus in Patristic, Medieval and Early Modern Traditions* (Leiden, 2005), p. 210.
26 Seán Ó Duinn, trans., *The Siege of Knocklong: Forbhais Droma Damhghaire* (Cork, 1992), p. 99. Available online at https://celt.ucc.ie.
27 Annie M. Scarre, trans. and ed., 'The Beheading of John the Baptist by Mog Ruith', *Ériu*, IV (1910), pp. 173–81.
28 Jeffrey Gantz, trans. and ed., *Early Irish Myths and Sagas* (London, 1981), p. 45.
29 Williams, *Ireland's Immortals*, p. 85.
30 Ibid., p. 93.
31 Gantz, *Early Irish Myths*, p. 175.
32 Whitley Stokes, trans. and ed., 'The Destruction of Dá Derga's Hostel', *Revue Celtique*, XXII (1901), pp. 14–61, p. 15.
33 Elizabeth Boyle, 'Allegory, the Áes Dána and the Liberal Arts in Medieval Irish Literature', in *Grammatica, Gramadach and Gramadeg: Vernacular Grammar and Grammarians in Medieval Ireland and Wales*, ed. Deborah Hayden and Paul Russell (Amsterdam, 2016), pp. 11–34.
34 Whitley Stokes, trans. and ed., 'The Irish Ordeals, Cormac's Adventure in the Land of Promise, and the Decision as to Cormac's Sword', in *Irische*

Texte mit Wörterbuch, ed. Ernste Windisch and Whitley Stokes (Leipzig, 1891), vol. IV, pp. 183–221. Available online at https://celt.ucc.ie.

35 James MacKillop, *Myths and Legends of the Celts* (London, 2005), pp. 55–7; Aldhouse-Green, *The Celtic Myths*, pp. 171–2; Williams, *Ireland's Immortals*, p. 23.

36 John Carey, *A Single Ray of the Sun: Religious Speculation in Early Ireland* (Aberystwyth, 2011), p. 20.

37 Williams, *Ireland's Immortals*, pp. 78–80.

38 Ibid., pp. 49–68.

39 Stokes, 'Cormac's Adventure', pp. 220–21.

40 Damian McManus, 'Good Looking and Irresistible: The Hero from Early Irish Saga to Classical Poetry', *Ériu*, LIX (2009), pp. 57–109, p. 61.

41 Alfred K. Siewers, 'Orthodoxy and Ecopoetics: The Green World in the Desert Sea', in *Toward an Ecology of Transfiguration: Orthodox Christian Perspectives on Environment, Nature and Creation*, ed. John Chryssavgis and Bruce V. Foltz (New York, 2013), pp. 243–62.

42 Gantz, *Early Irish Myths*, pp. 120–21.

43 Siewers, 'Orthodoxy and Ecopoetics', p. 250.

44 Jessica Hemming, 'Red, White and Black in Symbolic Thought: The Tricolour Folk Motif, Colour Naming, and Trichromatic Vision', *Folklore*, CXXIII/3 (2012), pp. 310–29, p. 312.

45 Giorgio Agamben, *Nudities*, trans. David Kishik and Stefan Pedatella (Stanford, CA, 2011), pp. 71–3.

46 Hemming, 'Red, White and Black', pp. 310–11.

47 Daibhi Ó Cróinín, *Early Medieval Ireland* (Oxford, 2016), pp. 252–8.

48 Lucas, 'The Sacred Trees of Ireland', p. 45.

49 Abram, *Myths of the Pagan North*, pp. 24–7.

50 Snorri Sturluson, *Edda*, trans. and ed. Anthony Faulkes (London, 1995), p. 18.

51 Ibid.

52 Abram, *Myths of the Pagan North*, pp. 127–31 and 149–51.

53 Ibid., p. 152.

54 Sarah Künzler, *Flesh and Word: Reading Bodies in Old Norse-Icelandic and Early Irish Literature* (Berlin, 2015), pp. 359–62; Margaret Clunies Ross, 'An Interpretation of the Myth of Þor's Encounter with Geirrøðr', in *Speculum Norroenum: Norse Studies in Memory of Gabriel Turville-Petre*, ed. Ursula Dronke et al. (Odense, 1981), pp. 370–92.

55 Clunies Ross, 'An Interpretation', p. 373.

56 Kevin Crossley-Holland, *The Penguin Book of Norse Myths: Gods of the Vikings* (London, 2018), pp. 220–21.

57 Abram, *Myths of the Pagan North*, pp. 155–7.

58 Julia H. McGrew and R. George Thomas, trans. and eds, *Sturlunga Saga: Shorter Sagas of the Icelanders* (New York, 1974), vol. II, p. 21.

59 Ibid., p. 22.

60 E.O.G. Turville-Petre, *Myth and Religion of the North: The Religion of Ancient Scandinavia* (New York, 1964), p. 98; Veikko Anttonen, 'Literary

Representation of Oral Religion: Organizing Principles in Mikael Agricola's List of Mythological Agents in Late Medieval Finland', in *More than Mythology: Narratives, Ritual Practices and Regional Distribution in Pre-Christian Scandinavian Religions*, ed. Catharina Raudvere and Jens Peter Schjødt (Lund, 2021), pp. 185–223, pp. 210–12.

61 Elias Lönnrot, *Kalevala*, trans. Keith Bosley (Oxford, 2008), p. 11.
62 Ibid., pp. 232–3.
63 Ibid., p. 304.

2 Magic and Medicine

1 Deborah J. Shepherd, 'A Brief Survey of Views on Christianisation in Karelia', *Russian History/Histoire Russe*, XXXII/3–4 (2005), pp. 491–511.
2 Veikko Anttonen, 'Literary Representation of Oral Religion: Organizing Principles in Mikael Agricola's List of Mythological Agents in Late Medieval Finland', in *More than Mythology: Narratives, Ritual Practices and Regional Distribution in Pre-Christian Scandinavian Religions*, ed. Catharina Raudvere and Jens Peter Schjødt (Lund, 2021), pp. 185–223.
3 Ibid., p. 186.
4 Charm quoted in Anniki Kaivola-Bregenhøj, *Riddles: Perspectives on the Use, Function and Change in a Folklore Genre* (Helsinki, 2001), p. 45.
5 Don Yoder, 'Toward a Definition of Folk Religion', *Western Folklore*, XXXIII/1 (1974), pp. 2–15.
6 Ronald Hutton, *Pagan Britain* (New Haven, CT, 2013), pp. 340–41; E. P. Thompson, *Customs in Common* (Pontypool, 2010), pp. 1–2.
7 David Elton Gay, 'On the Christianity of Incantations', in *Charms and Charming in Europe*, ed. Jonathan Roper (Basingstoke, 2004), pp. 32–58, pp. 32–4.
8 Laura Stark, *Peasants, Pilgrims and Sacred Promises: Ritual and the Supernatural in Orthodox Karelian Folk Religion* (Helsinki, 2002), p. 14. A useful summary of historical approaches can be found in Stuart Vyse, *Believing in Magic: The Psychology of Superstition* (Oxford, 2000), pp. 6–15.
9 Text and translation with commentary can be found in Godfrid Storms, *Anglo-Saxon Magic* (The Hague, 1948), pp. 172–86.
10 Michael D. J. Bintley, 'Brungen of Bearwe: Ploughing Common Furrows in Exeter Book Riddle 21, The Dream of the Rood, and the Æcerbot Charm', in *Trees and Timber in the Anglo-Saxon World*, ed. Michael D. J. Bintley and Michael G. Shapland (Oxford, 2013), pp. 144–57, p. 154. Hutton, *Pagan Britain*, pp. 336–9; Keith Thomas, *Religion and the Decline of Magic* (London, 1991), pp. 53–5.
11 Bruce A. Rosenberg, 'The Meaning of Æcerbot', *Journal of American Folklore*, LXXIX/313 (1966), pp. 428–36, p. 434.
12 Thomas D. Hill, 'The "Æcerbot" Charm and Its Christian User', *Anglo-Saxon England*, VI (1977), pp. 213–21, p. 213.
13 Rosenberg, 'Meaning of Æcerbot', pp. 430–31.
14 Bintley, 'Brungen of Bearwe', p. 155.

15 Hutton, *Pagan Britain*, p. 384. On the derivation of a gendered symbolism of creation and fertility from ancient philosophy, see Carolyn Merchant, *The Death of Nature: Women, Ecology and the Scientific Revolution* (New York, 1980), pp. 11–16.

16 Hill, 'The "Æcerbot" Charm', p. 218.

17 Ciaran Arthur, 'Ploughing through Cotton Caligula A. VII: Reading the Sacred Words of the *Heliand* and the *Æcerbot*', *Review of English Studies*, LXV/268 (2014), pp. 1–17, p. 4.

18 Rosenberg, 'Meaning of *Æcerbot*', p. 429.

19 Storms, *Anglo-Saxon Magic*, pp. 173 and 177.

20 R. Bovet, *Pandaemonium* [1684], ed. M. Summers (Aldington, 1951), p. 53, quoted in Thomas, *Religion and the Decline of Magic*, p. 649.

21 Ronald Hutton, *The Witch: A History of Fear from Ancient Times to the Present* (New Haven, CT, 2017), pp. 168–79. Thomas, *Religion and the Decline of Magic*, pp. 523–7.

22 Storms, *Anglo-Saxon Magic*, pp. 41–6.

23 Quoted in Henning Andersen, 'A Glimpse of the Homeland of the Slavs: Ecological and Cultural Change in Prehistory', in *Proceedings of the Seventh UCLA Indo-European Conference, Los Angeles 1995*, ed. Angela Della Volpe (Washington, DC, 1998), pp. 1–67 and 23–4. The text is translated from Wilhelm Lettenbauer, *Der Baumkult bei den Slaven* (Neuried, 1981).

24 A. N. Afanasyev, *The Poetic Outlook on Nature by the Slavs* [1865–9], quoted in Andersen, 'A Glimpse', p. 23.

25 Linda J. Ivanits, *Russian Folk Belief* (Abingdon, 1989), p. 35; Robin Milner-Gulland, *The Russians* (Oxford, 1997), p. 99.

26 Joanna Hubbs, *Mother Russia: The Feminine Myth in Russian Culture* (Bloomington, IN, 1983), pp. 118–23.

27 Rosenberg, 'Meaning of *Æcerbot*', p. 430; Andersen, 'A Glimpse', pp. 22–3.

28 Andersen, 'A Glimpse', p. 23.

29 Charms quoted in Ülo Valk, 'Thunder and Lightning in Estonian Folklore in the Light of Vernacular Theories', in *Mythic Discourses: Studies in Uralic Tradition*, ed. Frog, Anna-Leena Siikala and Eila Stepanova (Helsinki, 2012), pp. 40–67, p. 52.

30 Ibid.

31 Ülo Valk, 'The Devil's Identity: On the Problem of His Pre-Christian Prototype in Estonian Mythology', in *Myth and Mentality: Studies in Folklore and Popular Thought*, ed. Anna-Leena Siikala (Helsinki, 2002), pp. 122–8, p. 126.

32 Valdis Muktupāvels, 'Musical Instruments in the Baltic Region: Historiography and Traditions', *World of Music*, XLIV/3 (2002), pp. 21–54, p. 40.

33 Thomas Davidson, *Rowan Tree and Red Thread: A Scottish Witchcraft Miscellany of Tales, Legends and Ballads* (Edinburgh, 1949), p. 77.

34 King James I, *Daemonologie, In Form of a Dialogue Divided into Three Books* (1597). The text can be accessed online at www.gutenberg.org.

35 Julian Goodare, 'The Scottish Witchcraft Panic of 1597', in *The Scottish Witch-Hunt in Context*, ed. Julian Goodare (Manchester, 2002), pp. 51–72.

36 Anatoly Liberman, 'Out of Shakespeare: "Aroint Thee"', *Word Origins . . . and How We Know Them*, https://blog.oup.com, 20 February 2013.

37 Lizanne Henderson and Edward J. Cowan, *Scottish Fairy Belief: A History* (Edinburgh, 2001), p. 78.

38 'Elizabeth Maxwell', in *The Survey of Scottish Witchcraft Database*, https://witches.shca.ed.ac.uk, accessed 21 June 2022; James Rained, ed., *Depositions from the Castle of York, Relating to Offenses Committed in the Northern Counties in the Seventeenth Century* (Edinburgh, 1861).

39 Emma Wilby, *Cunning Folk and Familiar Spirits: Shamanistic Visionary Traditions in Early Modern British Witchcraft and Magic* (Brighton, 2005); Julian Goodare, 'The Cult of the Seely Wights in Scotland', *Folklore*, CXXIII/2 (2012), pp. 198–219.

40 See, for example, Silvia Federici, *Caliban and the Witch: Women, the Body and Primitive Accumulation* (Brooklyn, NY, 2014).

41 Sandra Modh, 'A Loop of Rowan Tree: Amulets Against Witchcraft', *England: The Other Within – Analysing the English Collections at the Pitt Rivers Museum*, https://england.prm.ox.ac.uk, accessed 18 October 2021.

42 Revd J. C. Atkinson, D.C.L., *Forty Years in a Moorland Parish: Reminiscences and Researches in Danby in Cleveland* (London, 1892), p. 97.

43 Ibid., p. 99.

44 Ronald Hutton, *The Stations of the Sun: A History of the Ritual Year in Britain* (Oxford, 1996), pp. 218–25.

45 John Lightfoot, *Flora Scotica; or, A Systematic Arrangement, in the Linnaean Method, of the Native Plants of Scotland and the Hebrides* (London, 1777), vol. 1, pp. 256–8.

46 Hutton, *Stations of the Sun*, p. 225.

47 Angela Bourke, *The Burning of Bridget Cleary* (London, 2006), p. 100.

48 Hutton, *The Witch*, pp. 249–50; Davidson, *Rowan Tree and Red Thread*, pp. 58–9.

49 Irish National Folklore Collection, Schools' Collection (NFCS) 1000: 156; informant unknown. Collector: Patrick Carolan, Virginia (B) School, Virginia, Co. Cavan. Teacher: E. O'Reilly. Available at www.duchas.ie.

50 NFCS 0991: 199–200; informant unknown. Collector: Bill Graham, Ballintemple School, Ballintemple, Co. Cavan. Teacher: S. Nic Eoin

51 NFCS 0961: 142; unnamed grandmother, aged 87. Collector: William McKenna, Cluain Cátha Schoold, Cloncaw, Co. Monaghan. Teacher: P. Ó Hanluain.

52 Amy-Jane Beer, *A Tree a Day* (London, 2021), p. 125; Richard Mabey, *Flora Britannica* (London, 1997), p. 203.

53 Sir James George Frazer, *The Golden Bough: A Study in Magic and Religion, a New Abridgement from the Second and Third Editions*, ed. Robert Fraser (Oxford, 1994), p. 795.

54 Ronald Black, ed., *The Gaelic Otherworld: John Gregorson Campbell's Superstitions of the Highlands and Islands of Scotland and Witchcraft and Second Sight in the Highlands and Islands* (Edinburgh, 2019), p. 17.

55 Ibid., p. 19.
56 Ronald Black, 'Introduction', in *The Gaelic Otherworld*, p. lvii.
57 Gordon Jarvie, 'Introduction', in *Scottish Folk and Fairy Tales from Burns to Buchan*, ed. Gordon Jarvie (London, 2008), pp. xi–xvii, p. xiii.
58 Stark, *Peasants, Pilgrims and Sacred Promises*, pp. 111–17.
59 Ibid., pp. 39–42.
60 Charm quoted in Juha Pentikäinen, *Oral Repertoire and Worldview* (Helsinki, 1978), p. 244.
61 Finnish Folklore Archive [*Suonen Kansan Vanhat Runot*], 11:773. Lupasalmi. 1884 – Jehkimä Putune, 65 years, quoted in Stark, *Peasants, Pilgrims and Sacred Promises*, p. 116.
62 Bourke, *Bridget Cleary*, p. 29.
63 Thomas, *Religion and the Decline of Magic*, pp. 670–77.
64 Lauren Martin, 'Witchcraft, Quarrels and Women's Work', in *The Scottish Witch-Hunt in Context*, ed. Goodare, pp. 73–89.
65 Black, ed., *The Gaelic Otherworld*, pp. xci–xcii.
66 Stark, *Peasants, Pilgrims and Sacred Promises*, p. 32. On the ideal of 'mutual obligation' in Highland society, see T. M. Devine, *The Scottish Clearances: A History of the Dispossessed* (London, 2018), pp. 22–3.

3 Arts of Nationhood

1 For information on how material for the Schools' Collection was collected, see Mícheál Briody, *The Irish Folklore Commission, 1935–1970: History, Ideology, Methodology* (Helsinki, 2016), pp. 264–7.
2 Irish National Folklore Collection, Schools' Collection (NFCS) 1113: 161–2. Collector: Mary Hegarty, Tullydush Upper, County Donegal. Teacher: Cathal P. Ó Lochlainn. Available online at www.duchas.ie/en.
3 Quoted in Briody, *The Irish Folklore Commission*, pp. 261–2.
4 John Hutchinson, *The Dynamics of Cultural Nationalism: The Gaelic Revival and the Creation of the Irish Nation State* (London, 1987), pp. 3–4.
5 See, for example, Eric Hobsbawm, *Nations and Nationalism Since 1780: Programme, Myth, Reality* (Cambridge, 1992), pp. 39–43; Benedict Anderson, *Imagined Communities: Reflections on the Origin and Spread of Nationalism* (London, 2016), pp. 33–46.
6 Caroline Baroness Nairne, *Lays from Strathearn* (Edinburgh, 1850), pp. 102–4.
7 Robert Archibald Smith, *The Scotish Minstrel: A Selection from the Vocal Melodies of Scotland, Ancient and Modern*, 6 vols (Edinburgh, 1821–4). Quoted in Karen E. McAuley, 'Minstrels of the Celtic Nations: Metaphors in Early Nineteenth-Century Celtic Song Collections', *Fontes Artis Musicae*, LIX/1 (2012), p. 29.
8 Johann Gottfried Herder, 'From *Alte Volkslieder / Ancient Folk Songs*', trans. Philip V. Bohlman, in *Song Loves the Masses: Herder on Music and Nationalism*, ed. Philip V. Bohlman (Oakland, CA, 2017), pp. 36 and 43.
9 Chris Bambery, *A People's History of Scotland* (London, 2018), pp. 56–9; Neil Davidson, *The Origins of Scottish Nationhood* (London, 2000), pp. 3–4.

10 William Donaldson, *The Jacobite Song: Political Myth and National Identity* (Aberdeen, 1988), p. 32.

11 Linda Colley, *Britons: Forging the Nation, 1707–1837* (New Haven, CT, 2005), pp. 11–13.

12 Freeland Barbour, *The White Rose of Gask: The Life and Songs of Carolina Oliphant, Lady Nairne* (Edinburgh, 2019), pp. 5–17.

13 T. M. Devine, *The Scottish Clearances: A History of the Dispossessed* (London, 2019), pp. 56–60.

14 Barbour, *White Rose of Gask*, pp. 33–5.

15 On the link between clanship and divine right, see Devine, *Scottish Clearances*, p. 50.

16 Tom Nairn, *The Break-Up of Britain: Crisis and Neo-Nationalism* (London, 1981), pp. 149–55.

17 See Katie Trumpener, *Bardic Nationalism: The Romantic Novel and the British Empire* (Princeton, NJ, 1997), p. 23.

18 George S. Christian, 'Gendering the Scottish Nation: Rereading the Songs of Lady Nairne', *European Romantic Review*, XXIX/6 (2019), pp. 681–709; Carol McGuirk, 'Jacobite History to National Song: Robert Burns and Carolina Oliphant (Baroness Nairne)', *Eighteenth Century*, LXVII/2–3 (2006), pp. 253–87.

19 W. B. Yeats, letter to Richard Le Gallienne, *c.* 15 October 1892, quoted in *Writings on Irish Folklore, Legend and Myth*, ed. Robert Welch (London, 1993), p. 415.

20 Hutchinson, *Dynamics of Cultural Nationalism*, pp. 130–34.

21 W. B. Yeats, *The Poems of W. B. Yeats*, vol. II: *1890–1898,* ed. Peter McDonald (London, 2021), pp. 175–6.

22 Roy Foster, *W. B. Yeats: A Life*, vol. II: *The Apprentice Mage, 1865–1914* (Oxford, 1998), p. 43.

23 Hutchinson, *Dynamics of Cultural Nationalism*, pp. 95–102.

24 Full story in Foster, *Yeats*, pp. 118–27.

25 Ibid., p. 131.

26 Mark Williams, *Ireland's Immortals: A History of the Gods of Irish Myth* (Princeton, NJ, 2016), pp. 332–46.

27 From Yeats's magical notebooks, quoted in Williams, *Ireland's Immortals*, p. 357.

28 George Russell, 'The Fountains of Youth', in *The Project Gutenberg E-Book of Æ in the Irish Theosophist* (2004), www.gutenberg.org.

29 John Sharkey, *Celtic Mysteries: The Ancient Religion* (London, 1975), pp. 82–3.

30 Anne Ross, *Pagan Celtic Britain* (London, 1992), pp. 48–55.

31 James MacKillop, *Myths and Legends of the Celts* (London, 2005), p. 11; Ross, *Pagan Celtic Britain*, p. 55.

32 Philip Marsden, *The Summer Isles: A Voyage of the Imagination* (London, 2019), pp. 31–2.

33 W. B. Yeats, 'The Celtic Element in Literature' [1898], in *Writings on Irish Folklore, Legend and Myth*, ed. Welch, p. 199.

34 Ibid., p. 191.

35 Glenda Dawn Goss, 'A Backdrop for the Young Sibelius: The Intellectual Genesis of the Kullervo Symphony', *19th-Century Music*, XXVII/1 (2003), pp. 48–73.

36 Ibid., p. 68; Ville Lukkarinen, 'Native Land, Art and Landscape in Finland in the Late 19th and 20th Centuries', in *Nordic Dawn: Modernism's Awakening in Finland, 1890–1920*, ed. Stephan Koja (London, 2005), pp. 26–8.

37 Lukkarinen, 'Native Land', pp. 30–31.

38 Ville Lukkarinen, 'Art and National Identity: Finland at the Turn of the Nineteenth and Twentieth Centuries', in *Northern Stars and Southern Lights: The Golden Age of Finnish Art, 1870–1920*, ed. Adriaan E. Waiboer (Dublin, 2008), p. 15.

39 Elias Lönnrot, *Kalevala*, trans. Keith Bosley (Oxford, 2008), p. 444.

4 Romantic Ecologies

1 Mary Lutyens, *Millais and the Ruskins* (London, 1967), p. 75. See also Alastair Grieve, 'Ruskin and Millais at Glenfinlas', *Burlington Magazine*, CXXXVIII/1117 (1996), pp. 228–34, and Phyllis Rose, *Parallel Lives: Five Victorian Marriages* (London, 2020), pp. 45–100.

2 John Ruskin, letter to his parents, 13 July 1853, quoted in 'Introduction', in *The Works of John Ruskin*, vol. XII: *Lectures on Architecture and Painting*, ed. E. T. Cook and Alexander Wedderburn, 39 vols (London, 1903–12), p. xx. The entire text is available for PDF download online at www.lancaster.ac.uk. Hereafter cited as *Works* (vol.).

3 John Ruskin, letter to his father, 6 July 1853, quoted in *Works* (vol. XII), p. xxiv; John Ruskin, letter to Lady Trevelyan, 6 September 1853, in *Reflections of a Friendship: John Ruskin's Letters to Pauline Trevelyan, 1848–1866*, ed. Virginia Surtees (London, 1979), p. 57.

4 Lutyens, *Millais and the Ruskins*, p. 75.

5 Jason Rosenfeld, *John Everett Millais* (London, 2012), pp. 36–8.

6 Grieve, 'Millais at Glenfinlas', p. 228.

7 Ruskin, letter to Dr Furnivall, 16 October 1853, quoted in *Works* (vol. XII), p. xxiv.

8 Ruskin, letter to his father, 28 July 1853, quoted in Lutyens, *Millais and the Ruskins*, p. 75.

9 Samuel Taylor Coleridge, 'The Picture; or, The Lover's Resolution', first published in the *Morning Post*, 6 September 1802. See Richard Holmes, *Coleridge: Early Visions* (London, 2005), pp. 323 and 333.

10 William Wordsworth, *The Poetical Works of William Wordsworth*, ed. William Knight (London, 1896), vol. V, p. 313.

11 Richard Mabey, *The Cabaret of Plants: Botany and the Imagination* (London, 2015), p. 7.

12 Rosenfeld, *Millais*, p. 33.

13 Ibid., p. 80.

14 Millais, letter to Combe, quoted in Ruskin, *Works* (vol. XII), p. xxviii. On Holman Hunt and Ruskin, see Robert Hewison, 'A New and Noble

School in England: Ruskin and the Pre-Raphaelites', in 'A New and Noble School': Ruskin and the Pre-Raphaelites, Ruskin's Complete Writings on the Pre-Raphaelites, ed. Stephen Wildman (London, 2012), pp. 17–33, pp. 20–22.

15 Ibid., pp. 22–5.

16 Rosenfeld, Millais, pp. 24–7.

17 Robert Hewison, John Ruskin: The Argument of the Eye (London, 1976), pp. 36–50.

18 John Ruskin, 'Pre-Raphaelitism' (lecture delivered on 18 November 1853), in Wildman, ed., Complete Writings on the Pre-Raphaelites, pp. 109–33; for Ruskin on art education, see Robert Hewison, '"The Teaching of Art Is the Teaching of All Things": Ruskin, Sight and Insight', in Ruskin and His Contemporaries (London, 2018), pp. 171–86.

19 Ruskin, 'Pre-Raphaelitism', p. 121.

20 Ruskin, Works (vol. III, Modern Painters I), p. 624.

21 Ruskin, 'Pre-Raphaelitism', in Wildman, ed., Complete Writings on the Pre-Raphaelites, pp. 80–81.

22 Quotations from Works (vol. III, Modern Painters I), pp. 476, 556 and 590.

23 John Ruskin, Works (vol. XXV, Love's Meinie and Proserpina), p. 356.

24 John Ruskin, Works (vol. XXXV, Praeterita), pp. 314–15.

25 Robert Hewison, '"The Mind Revolts": Ruskin and Darwin', in Ruskin and His Contemporaries, pp. 279–305.

26 John Ruskin, 'The Nature of Gothic', in Unto This Last and Other Writings, ed. Clive Wilmer (London, 1997), pp. 103–4.

27 On Ruskin's biophilia and the story of his ideas about plants, see M. M. Mahood, 'Ruskin's Flowers of Evil', in The Poet as Botanist (Cambridge, 2008), pp. 147–82, p. 153.

28 John Ruskin, Works (vol. IV, Modern Painters II), p. 147.

29 Ibid., p. 154.

30 Hewison, Argument of the Eye, p. 18.

31 Carol Kyros Walker, 'Introduction', in Dorothy Wordsworth, Recollections of a Tour Made in Scotland, ed. Carol Kyros Walker (New Haven, CT, 1997), pp. 1–3.

32 Robert Macfarlane, Mountains of the Mind: A History of a Fascination (London, 2003), pp. 14–15; Simon Schama, Landscape and Memory (London, 1995), pp. 411–23.

33 Schama, Landscape and Memory, pp. 447–50.

34 John Barrell, The Idea of Landscape and the Sense of Place, 1730–1840 (Cambridge, 1972), p. 4.

35 Ibid., pp. 5–12.

36 Jonathan Bate, 'The Picturesque Environment', in The Song of the Earth (London, 2000), pp. 119–52.

37 Robert Burns, 'The Humble Petition of Bruar Water', in The Complete Poems and Songs of Robert Burns (Glasgow, 2000), p. 210.

38 Dorothy Wordsworth, Recollections, pp. 167–8.

39 The story is told on the Atholl Estates website: 'Woodland Lodges', https://atholl-estates.co.uk, accessed 1 August 2022.

40 Peter Dale and Brandon C. Yen, *Wordsworth's Garden and Flowers: The Spirit of Paradise* (Woodbridge, 2018), p. 71.

41 Barrell, *The Idea of Landscape*, p. 7.

42 William Gilpin, *Remarks on Forest Scenery and Other Woodland Views* (London, 1791), vol. I, pp. 38–9.

43 Bate, 'Picturesque Environment', p. 136.

44 Tom Williamson, 'Grass, Wood and Water: Approaches to the Ecology of Brown's Landscapes', in *What Did Capability Brown Do for Ecology?*, ed. Ian D. Rotherham and Christine Handley (Sheffield, 2017), pp. 141–66, p. 153.

45 Dorothy Wordsworth, *The Grasmere and Alfoxden Journals*, ed. Pamela Woof (Oxford, 2002), pp. 90–91.

46 William Wordsworth, 'Farewell, Thou Little Nook of Mountain Ground', in *The Major Works*, ed. Stephen Gill (Oxford, 2000), pp. 278–9.

47 Richard Mabey, *Weeds: The Story of Outlaw Plants* (London, 2012), pp. 5–14.

48 Judith W. Page, 'Dorothy Wordsworth's "Gratitude to Insensate Things": Gardening in "The Grasmere Journals"', *Wordsworth Circle*, XXXIX/1–2 (2008), pp. 19–23, p. 22.

49 Dale and Yen, *Wordsworth's Gardens*, p. 47. For a list of plants at Dove Cottage and a contemporary description, by Wordsworth's nephew, of the garden at Rydal Mount, see Carol Buchanan, *Wordsworth's Gardens* (Lubbock, 2001), pp. 199–206.

50 William Wordsworth, *The Major Works*, p. 584.

51 John Ruskin, 'Unto This Last', in *Unto This Last and Other Writings*, p. 222.

52 Ibid.

53 Rosenfeld, *Millais*, p. 200.

54 A. Savinov, 'Shishkin as a Painter', in *Ivan Shishkin: Paintings, Graphic Works*, ed. Irina Shuvalova (Leningrad, 1986), p. 6.

55 Christopher Ely, *This Meager Nature: Landscape and National Identity in Imperial Russia* (DeKalb, IL, 2009), p. 187.

56 Shuvalova, ed., *Ivan Shishkin*, p. ii.

5 Other Russias

1 Walter Benjamin, 'The Storyteller: Reflections on the Works of Nikolai Leskov', in *Illuminations*, ed. Hannah Arendt, trans. Harry Zorn (London, 1999), pp. 83–107, p. 84.

2 Karl Marx and Friedrich Engels, *The Communist Manifesto*, ed. Gareth Stedman Jones (London, 2002), p. 223.

3 V. I. Lenin, 'Letters from Afar', in *Lenin Collected Works*, trans. M. S. Levin (Moscow, 1964), vol. XXIII, unpaginated, available at www.marxists.org.

4 Orlando Figes, *A People's Tragedy: The Russian Revolution* (London, 2017), pp. 384–8.

5 Viktoria Schweitzer, *Tsvetaeva*, ed. Angela Livingstone, trans. Robert Chandler and H. T. Willetts (London, 1992), pp. 6–7.

6 Marina Tsvetaeva, *Milestones*, trans. Christopher Whyte (Bristol, 2015), p. 61.

7 Marina Tsvetaeva, *Earthly Signs: Moscow Diaries 1917–1922*, trans. and ed. Jamey Gambrell (New York, 2002).

8 Tara Bergin, Marina Tsvetkova and Christopher Whyte, 'Looking for/ Longing for/ Sick for Home: Marina Tsvetaeva in English Translation', *Translation and Literature*, XXIII/3 (2014), pp. 336–63.

9 Svetlana Boym, *The Future of Nostalgia* (New York, 2001), p. 12.

10 All quotations in this paragraph are from Christopher Whyte's translation of the poem, found in Bergin et al., 'Tsvetaeva in English Translation', p. 362. See also Marina Tsvetaeva, *Bride of Ice: New Selected Poems,* trans. Elaine Feinstein (Manchester, 2009), pp. 133–4.

11 Angela Livingstone, 'Introduction', in Marina Tsvetaeva, *Art in the Light of Conscience: Eight Essays on Poetry*, trans. Angela Livingstone (Hexham, 2010), pp. 2–3.

12 Orlando Figes, *Natasha's Dance: A Cultural History of Russia* (London, 2002), p. 527.

13 Bergin et al., 'Tsvetaeva in English Translation', p. 356.

14 Tsvetaeva, *Milestones*, p. 61.

15 Schweitzer, *Tsvetaeva*, pp. 227–32.

16 Quotations from 'Trees' are from Marina Tsvetaeva, *After Russia: The First Notebook*, trans. Christopher Whyte (Bristol, 2017), pp. 66–74.

17 Figes, *Natasha's Dance*, p. 528.

18 Ibid., pp. 568–78; Schweitzer, *Tsvetaeva*, pp. 326–39 and 348–72.

19 Quoted in Christopher Whyte, 'Introduction', in Tsvetaeva, *After Russia*, pp. 25–6.

20 Quoted in Schweitzer, *Tsvetaeva*, p. 230.

21 Guy de Mallac, *Boris Pasternak: His Life and Art* (London, 1983), pp. 221–57.

22 Ibid., p. 332; I. A. Esaulov, 'The Paschal Archetype of Russian Literature and the Structure of Boris Pasternak's Novel *Doctor Zhivago*', trans. Margaret Tejerizo, *Literature and Theology*, XX/I (2006), pp. 63–78, p. 67.

23 Boris Pasternak, *Doctor Zhivago*, trans. Richard Pevear and Larissa Volokhonsky (London, 2010), pp. 8–9.

24 Ibid., p. 38.

25 Mallac, *Pasternak*, pp. 307–9.

26 Pasternak, *Zhivago*, p. 303.

27 Ibid., pp. 335–6.

28 Per-Arne Bodin, 'Boris Pasternak and the Christian Tradition', *Forum for Modern Language Studies*, XXVI/4 (1990), pp. 382–401; Martha M. F. Kelly, 'Cultural Transformation as Transdisfiguration in Pasternak's *Doctor Zhivago*', *Russian History*, XI/I (2013), pp. 68–89. On the connection of Sophia to pagan nature divinities, see Joanna Hubbs, *Mother Russia: The Feminine Myth in Russian Culture* (Bloomington, IN, 1988), pp. 101–5.

29 Pasternak, *Zhivago*, p. 317.

30 Hubbs, *Mother Russia*, p. 207.

31 Leo Tolstoy, *War and Peace*, trans. Rosemary Edmonds (Harmondsworth, 1978), p. 497.

32 F. T. Griffiths and S. J. Rabinowitz, 'Doctor Zhivago and the Tradition of National Epic', *Comparative Literature*, XXXII/1 (1980), pp. 63–79, p. 76.
33 George Eliot, *Middlemarch*, ed. W. J. Harvey (London, 1965), p. 896.
34 Pasternak, *Zhivago*, p. 414.

6 Uprootings

1 Basil Bunting, *The Poems of Basil Bunting*, ed. Don Share (London, 2016), pp. 94–5.
2 Ibid., pp. 386–7.
3 David Craig and David Paterson, *The Glens of Silence: Landscapes of the Highland Clearances* (Edinburgh, 2004), pp. 115–16; Robert Macfarlane, *The Wild Places* (London, 2007), pp. 123–4.
4 Somhairle MacGill-Eain/Sorley MacLean, *Caoir Gheal Leumraich White Leaping Flame: Collected Poems in Gaelic with English Translations*, ed. Christopher Whyte and Emma Dymock (Edinburgh, 2011), p. 470.
5 Sorley MacLean, *Poems*, pp. 230–34.
6 Steve Chettle, 'Introduction', in Andy Goldsworthy, *Sheepfolds* (London, 1996), pp. 7–9.
7 James Putnam, 'Introduction', in Andy Goldsworthy, *Enclosure* (London, 2007), pp. 9–14.
8 All quotations in this paragraph from Andy Goldsworthy, *Enclosure*, pp. 126–9.
9 Andy Goldsworthy, *Andy Goldsworthy* (London, 1990), unpaginated.
10 Ibid.
11 Thierry de Duve, *Kant After Duchamp* (London, 1996), pp. 175–91.
12 Anita Albus, *The Art of Arts: Rediscovering Painting*, trans. Michael Robertson (London, 2001), pp. 65–74; Michael Taussig, *What Colour Is the Sacred?* (Chicago, IL, 2009), pp. 41–5.
13 Albus, *Art of Arts*, p. 276.
14 Goldsworthy, *Goldsworthy*, unpaginated.
15 William Malpas, *The Art of Andy Goldsworthy* (Maidstone, 2007), pp. 63–4 and 92.
16 Grevel Lindop, 'Editorial Introduction', in Robert Graves, *The White Goddess*, ed. Grevel Lindop (London, 1997), pp. xvi–xxi.
17 Ronald Hutton, *The Triumph of the Moon: A History of Modern Pagan Witchcraft* (Oxford, 1999), pp. 41–2 and 188–94.
18 Graves, *White Goddess*, p. 20.
19 Ibid., pp. 162–3.
20 George Calder, ed., *Auraicept Na N-éces: The Scholars' Primer: Being the Texts of the Ogham Tract from the Book of Ballymote and the Yellow Book of Lecan, and the Text of the Trefhocul from the Book of Leinster* (Edinburgh, 1917), p. 91. Full text available online at https://celt.ucc.ie.
21 Graves, *White Goddess*, p. 10.
22 Seamus Heaney, *Opened Ground: Poems, 1966–1996* (London, 1998), p. 181.

23 Brian Keeble, *These Bright Shadows: The Poetry of Kathleen Raine* (New York, 2020), p. 57.

24 Kathleen Raine, *Autobiographies* (London, 1991), pp. 6–8.

25 Kathleen Jamie, 'Diary: In the West Highlands', *London Review of Books*, XXXIII/14 (14 July 2011).

26 Raine, *Autobiographies*, p. 270.

27 Ibid., p. 271.

28 Kathleen Raine, *Collected Poems* (London, 2019), pp. 65–7.

29 Raine, *Autobiographies*, pp. 272–4.

30 Ibid., p. 287.

31 Raine, *Collected Poems*, p. 132.

32 Ibid.

33 Raine, *Autobiographies*, p. 311.

34 Raine, *Collected Poems*, p. 215. Italics in original.

Conclusion: Where One Tree Survives

1 'Tree of the Year: Scots Rowan to Represent Great Britain in European Event', BBC News, www.bbc.co.uk, 7 December 2020; see also Tree of the Year, www.treeoftheyear.org.

2 Myrtle Ashmole and Philip Ashmole, eds, *The Carrifran Wildwood Story* (Jedburgh, 2009), pp. 72–5. As the editors inform us, this section of the book is 'based on information kindly provided by Derek Robeson, Elizabeth Pickett and Steve Hannah'.

3 Ibid., p. 34.

4 Ann Goodburn, 'People in Historic Times', ibid., pp. 58–63.

5 On headage payments, see Mark Cocker, *Our Place: Can We Save Britain's Wildlife Before It Is Too Late?* (London, 2018), p. 215. On 'unwanted vegetation', see George Monbiot, *Feral: Rewilding the Land, Sea and Human Life* (London, 2014), p. 161.

6 'Reviving the Wild Heart of Southern Scotland', Borders Forest Trust, www.bordersforesttrust.org, accessed 4 October 2021.

7 Cocker, *Our Place*, pp. 169 and 249–51.

8 Alan Watson Featherstone, 'The Wonder Tree', https://alanwatsonfeatherstone.com, 1 September 2003.

9 Ashmole and Ashmole, eds, *The Carrifran Wildwood Story*, p. 47.

10 Fi Martynoga, 'Prehistoric People', in *The Carrifran Wildwood Story*, ed. Ashmole and Ashmole, pp. 57–8.

11 Philip Ashmole and Richard Tipping, 'The Peat Core from Rotten Bottom – A Unique Record of a Changing Environment', in *The Carrifran Wildwood Story*, ed. Ashmole and Ashmole, pp. 76–80.

12 Stuart Adair, 'The Nature of the Wild Heart', in *A Journey in Landscape Restoration: Carrifran Wildwood and Beyond*, ed. Myrtle Ashmole and Philip Ashmole (Dunbeath, 2020), pp. 116–17.

13 Ronald Hutton, *Pagan Britain* (New Haven, CT, 2013), p. 31.

14 Ashmole and Ashmole, eds, *The Carrifran Wildwood Story*, pp. 117–22.

15 Stuart Adair, 'Vegetation Released from Domestic Grazing', in *A Journey in Landscape Restoration*, ed. Ashmole and Ashmole, pp. 26–46.

16 Philip Ashmole, Myrtle Ashmole and Stuart Adair, 'Return of the Flowers: A Restoration Gallery', in *A Journey in Landscape Restoration*, ed. Ashmole and Ashmole, pp. 47–64.

17 John Savory, 'Birds as Indicators of Environmental Change at Carrifran', in *A Journey in Landscape Restoration*, ed. Ashmole and Ashmole, pp. 65–79.

18 George Monbiot, 'Everything is Connected', in *How Did We Get into this Mess?: Politics, Equality, Nature* (London, 2016), pp. 79–87; Monbiot, *Feral*, p. 107.

19 Monbiot, *Feral*, pp. 81–3.

20 Philip Ashmole and Stuart Adair, 'Nature Still Needs a Hand at Carrifran', in *A Journey in Landscape Restoration*, ed. Ashmole and Ashmole, pp. 97–104.

21 Norman MacCaig, *The Poems of Norman MacCaig*, ed. Ewan MacCaig (Edinburgh, 2005), p. 351.

22 Colin N. Waters et al., 'The Anthropocene is Functionally and Stratigraphically Distinct from the Holocene', *Science*, CCCII/6269 (2016), p. 137.

23 Cocker, *Our Place*, p. 247.

24 George Peterken, *Meadows* (Oxford, 2013), pp. 357–61; Cocker, *Our Place*, p. 159.

25 'State of Nature 2019 Infographics', NBN, https://nbn.org.uk, accessed 4 October 2021.

26 Samantha Walton, *Everybody Needs Beauty: In Search of the Nature Cure* (London, 2021), pp. 83–116.

27 Jenny Odell, *How to Do Nothing: Resisting the Attention Economy* (New York and London, 2019), pp. 148–52.

28 Jessie Sheeler, *Little Sparta: The Garden of Ian Hamilton Finlay* (London, 2003), pp. 15–17.

29 Alec Finlay, ed., *Ian Hamilton Finlay: Selections* (London, 2012), p. 179.

30 John Dixon Hunt, *Nature Over Again: The Garden Art of Ian Hamilton Finlay* (London, 2008), pp. 75–80.

31 The formulation of this thought follows Rebecca Tamás, 'On Pansychism', in *Strangers: Essays on the Human and Nonhuman* (London, 2020), pp. 41–52.

Further Reading

Ashmole, Myrtle, and Philip Ashmole, eds, *The Carrifran Wildwood Story* (Jedburgh, 2009)

—, *A Journey in Landscape Restoration: Carrifran Wildwood and Beyond* (Dunbeath, 2020)

Barbour, Freeland, *The White Rose of Gask: The Life and Songs of Carolina Oliphant, Lady Nairne* (Edinburgh, 2019)

Barrell, John, *The Idea of Landscape and the Sense of Place, 1730–1840* (Cambridge, 1972)

Bate, Jonathan, *The Song of the Earth* (London, 2000)

Beer, Amy-Jane, *A Tree a Day* (London, 2021)

Black, Ronald, ed., *The Gaelic Otherworld: John Gregorson Campbell's Superstitions of the Highlands and Islands of Scotland and Witchcraft and Second Sight in the Highlands and Islands* (Edinburgh, 2019)

Bunting, Basil, *The Poems of Basil Bunting*, ed. Don Share (London, 2016)

Craig, David, and David Paterson, *The Glens of Silence: Landscapes of the Highland Clearances* (Edinburgh, 2004)

Dale, Peter, and Brandon C. Yen, *Wordsworth's Garden and Flowers: The Spirit of Paradise* (Woodbridge, 2018)

Davidson, Thomas, *Rowan Tree and Red Thread: A Scottish Witchcraft Miscellany of Tales, Legends and Ballads* (Edinburgh, 1949)

Donaldson, William, *The Jacobite Song: Political Myth and National Identity* (Aberdeen, 1988)

Evelyn, John, *Sylva; or, A Discourse of Forest Trees* (London, 1664)

Featherstone, Alan Watson, 'The Wonder Tree', www.alanwatsonfeatherstone.com, 1 September 2003

Figes, Orlando, *Natasha's Dance: A Cultural History of Russia* (London, 2002)

Foster, Roy, *W. B. Yeats: A Life*, vol. I: *The Apprentice Mage, 1865–1914* (Oxford, 1998)

Gantz, Jeffrey, trans. and ed., *Early Irish Myths and Sagas* (London, 1981)

Graves, Robert, *The White Goddess*, ed. Grevel Lindop (London, 1997)

Grigson, Geoffrey, *The Englishman's Flora* (St Albans, 1958)

Hewison, Robert, *John Ruskin: The Argument of the Eye* (London, 1976)

Howkins, Chris, *Rowan: Tree of Protection* (Addlestone, 1996)

Hubbs, Joanna, *Mother Russia: The Feminine Myth in Russian Culture* (Bloomington, IN, 1983)

Hutchinson, John, *The Dynamics of Cultural Nationalism: The Gaelic Revival and the Creation of the Irish Nation State* (London, 1987)

Hutton, Ronald, *Blood and Mistletoe: The History of the Druids in Britain* (New Haven, CT, 2009)

—, *The Stations of the Sun: A History of the Ritual Year in Britain* (Oxford, 1996)

—, *The Witch: A History of Fear from Ancient Times to the Present* (New Haven, CT, 2017)

Goldsworthy, Andy, *Andy Goldsworthy* (London, 1990)

—, *Enclosure* (London, 2007)

—, *Sheepfolds* (London, 1996)

Joyce, P. W., trans. and ed., *Old Celtic Romances* (London, 1879)

Koch, John T., and John Carey, eds, *The Celtic Heroic Age: Literary Sources for Ancient Celtic Europe and Early Ireland and Wales* (Aberystwyth, 2003)

Koja, Stephan, ed., *Nordic Dawn: Modernism's Awakening in Finland, 1890–1920* (London, 2005)

Lightfoot, John, *Flora Scotica; or, A Systematic Arrangement, in the Linnaean Method, of the Native Plants of Scotland and the Hebrides* (London, 1777)

Lönnrot, Elias, *Kalevala*, trans. Keith Bosley (Oxford, 2008)

Lucas, A. T., 'The Sacred Trees of Ireland', *Journal of the Cork Historical and Archaeological Society*, LXVIII/207–8 (1963), pp. 46–7

Lutyens, Mary, *Millais and the Ruskins* (London, 1967)

Mabey, Richard, *The Cabaret of Plants: Botany and the Imagination* (London, 2015)

—, *Flora Britannica* (London, 1997)

McAllister, Hugh, *The Genus Sorbus: Mountain Ash and Other Rowans* (Kew, 2005)

MacCaig, Norman, *The Poems of Norman MacCaig*, ed. Ewan MacCaig (Edinburgh, 2005)

MacCoitir, Niall, *Irish Trees. Myths, Legends and Folklore* (Cork, 2003)

MacGill-Eain, Somhairle (Sorley MacLean), *Caoir Gheal Leumraich/White Leaping Flame: Collected Poems in Gaelic with English Translations*, ed. Christopher Whyte and Emma Dymock (Edinburgh, 2011)

MacKillop, James, *Myths and Legends of the Celts* (London, 2005)

Mallac, Guy, *Boris Pasternak: His Life and Art* (London, 1983)

Modh, Sandra, 'A Loop of Rowan Tree: Amulets Against Witchcraft', *England: The Other Within – Analysing the English Collections at the Pitt Rivers Museum*, https://england.prm.ox.ac.uk

Monbiot, George, *Feral: Rewilding the Land, Sea and Human Life* (London, 2014)

Odell, Jenny, *How to Do Nothing: Resisting the Attention Economy* (New York and London, 2019)

Pasternak, Boris, *Doctor Zhivago*, trans. Richard Pevear and Larissa Volokhonsky (London, 2010)

Pastoureau, Michel, *Red: The History of a Color* (Princeton, NJ, 2017)

Raine, Kathleen, *Autobiographies* (London, 1991)

—, *Collected Poems* (London, 2019)

Rosenfeld, Jason, *John Everett Millais* (London, 2012)

Ross, Anne, *Folklore of the Scottish Highlands* (Stroud, 2011)
—, *Pagan Celtic Britain* (London, 1992)
Ruskin, John, *The Stones of Venice*; *Modern Painters*, vols I, II and V; *Proserpina* —
    all available for PDF download as part of *The Works of John Ruskin*,
    ed. E. T. Cook and Alexander Wedderburn, 39 vols (London, 1903–12),
    www.lancaster.ac.uk
Russell, George, 'The Fountains of Youth', in *The Project Gutenberg E-Book
    of Æ in the Irish Theosophist* (2004), www.gutenberg.org
Schweitzer, Viktoria, *Tsvetaeva*, ed. Angela Livingstone, trans. Robert Chandler
    and H. T. Willetts (London, 1992)
Sheeler, Jessie, *Little Sparta: The Garden of Ian Hamilton Finlay* (London, 2003)
Shuvalova, Irina, ed., *Ivan Shishkin: Paintings, Graphic Works* (Leningrad, 1986)
Snorri Sturluson, *Edda*, trans. and ed. Anthony Faulkes (London, 1995)
Stafford, Fiona, *The Long, Long Life of Trees* (New Haven, CT, 2016)
Stark, Laura, *Peasants, Pilgrims and Sacred Promises: Ritual and the Supernatural in
    Orthodox Karelian Folk Religion* (Helsinki, 2002)
Storms, Godfrid, *Anglo-Saxon Magic* (The Hague, 1948)
Tamás, Rebecca, *Strangers: Essays on the Human and Nonhuman* (London, 2020)
Thomas, Keith, *Religion and the Decline of Magic* (London, 1991)
Tsvetaeva, Marina, *After Russia: The First Notebook*, trans. Christopher Whyte
    (Bristol, 2017)
—, *Bride of Ice: New Selected Poems,* trans. Elaine Feinstein (Manchester, 2009)
—, *Milestones*, trans. Christopher Whyte (Bristol, 2015)
Wilby, Emma, *Cunning Folk and Familiar Spirits: Shamanistic Visionary Traditions in
    Early Modern British Witchcraft and Magic* (Brighton, 2005)
Williams, Mark, *Ireland's Immortals: A History of the Gods of Irish Myth* (Princeton,
    NJ, 2016)
Wordsworth, Dorothy, *The Grasmere and Alfoxden Journals*, ed. Pamela Woof
    (Oxford, 2002)
—, *Recollections of a Tour Made in Scotland*, ed. Carol Kyros Walker (New Haven,
    CT, 1997)
Wordsworth, William, *The Major Works*, ed. Stephen Gill (Oxford, 2000)
Yashin, Alexander, 'A Feast of Rowanberries', in *We the Russians: Voices from
    Russia*, ed. Colette Shulman (New York, 1972)
Yeats, W. B., *The Poems of W. B. Yeats*, vol. II: *1890–1898*, ed. Peter McDonald
    (London, 2021)
—, *Writings on Irish Folklore, Legend and Myth*, ed. Robert Welch (London, 1993)

Associations and Websites

BORDERS FOREST TRUST
Carrifran Wildwood and other ecological restoration projects
https://bordersforesttrust.org

CORPUS OF ELECTRONIC TEXTS
Thousands of open-access Irish texts
https://celt.ucc.ie

EUROPEAN TREE OF THE YEAR
www.treeoftheyear.org

GALLEN-KALLELA MUSEUM
Searchable images and archival material
www.gallen-kallela.fi

IRISH NATIONAL FOLKLORE COLLECTION
Database of Irish folklore
www.duchas.ie

LITTLE SPARTA
Explore the garden online
www.littlesparta.org.uk

MUSEUM OF MAGIC AND WITCHCRAFT
Searchable archive of magical objects and texts
https://museumofwitchcraftandmagic.co.uk

NESS BOTANIC GARDENS
Extensive collection of rowans
www.liverpool.ac.uk/ness-gardens

PITT RIVERS MUSEUM
Searchable artefact collections with images
www.prm.ox.ac.uk

THE RUSKIN LIBRARY
Includes access to *Complete Works*
www.lancaster.ac.uk/the-ruskin

SHEEPFOLDS
Information on Andy Goldsworthy's *Sheepfolds* project
www.sheepfoldscumbria.co.uk

SURVEY OF SCOTTISH WITCHCRAFT
Interactive database of historic witch trials
www.shca.ed.ac.uk/Research/witches

WORDSWORTH GRASMERE
Information on Dove Cottage and the Wordsworth archives
https://wordsworth.org.uk

Acknowledgements

Since the contract for *Rowan* was signed during the first lockdown of 2020, much of the research for the book had to be conducted from home. Profound thanks to the libraries, museums and archives who make images and texts freely available online and to the many people who share images on sites like Geograph and Wikimedia Commons. Such resources enrich the possibilities of imaginative travel, especially when physical movement is severely circumscribed.

Mark Williams, Jacqueline Borsje and Maxim Fomin all generously assisted my research into early Irish literature by suggesting sources, sharing my questions with colleagues and offering clarifications on the language of the texts. Leo, at Rydal Mount, answered my questions about rowan in the gardens there. Fiona Love, from Borders Forest Trust, responded almost instantly to my emailed enquiries about Carrifran and put me in touch with Philip Ashmole, one of the founding members. Philip kindly spoke to me by phone about rowan in the Scottish Borders, sharing numerous insights into the tree's ecology. It was a privilege to have this glimpse of his enthusiasm and knowledge about woods and trees. He also provided some wonderful photographs. Christopher Whyte offered invaluable criticism of my work on Tsvetaeva, kindly granting permission to use his translations of the poems. A conversation with Sasha Dugdale helped bring Tsvetaeva's singular poetics more sharply into focus. Orlando Reade's online Wordsworth seminar provided a welcome community during lockdown and rich inspiration for 'Romantic Ecologies'.

A few people have consistently read *Rowan* as it evolved in draft. Catherine Crocker has been one of my most supportive readers. My parents greeted each new chapter as if it were the next instalment of a gripping serial. I thank them for their love and support.

Anna Moser read this numerous times, improving the writing and thinking at every stage; she calmed my worries about wordcounts, gathered and catalogued images with me, and listened to me witter about rowans for months. I look forward to returning the favour.

Photo Acknowledgements

The author and publishers wish to express their thanks to the below sources of illustrative material and/or permission to reproduce it. Some locations of artworks are also given below, in the interest of brevity:

Alamy Stock Photo: pp. 22 (Paul Wood), 33 (Interfoto), 117 (Michael Grubka), 154 (robertharding, photo Philip Craven), 162 (Evgeny Drobzhev), 192–3 (Neil Dangerfield), 196 (Duncan Astbury); © Jean-Jacques Alcalay/Biosphoto: pp. 26–7; photos Philip Ashmole, reproduced with permission: pp. 200, 208, 209; Ashmolean Museum, University of Oxford: p. 132; © The Board of Trinity College Dublin: p. 55 (MS 58, fol. 292r); courtesy Borders Forest Trust: p. 203; © 2021 Buyrussiangifts/Theambergiftshop, reproduced with permission: p. 169; Chazen Museum of Art, Madison, WI: p. 114 (photo Daderot, public domain); collection of the author: p. 178; Dulwich Picture Gallery, London: p. 141; Finnish National Gallery, Helsinki: pp. 125, 126, 129; Flickr: pp. 52 (photo Abi Skipp, CC BY 2.0), 92 (Culture Vannin, public domain); Geograph Britain and Ireland: pp. 16 (photo Claire Pegrum, CC BY-SA 2.0), 153 (photo Jonathan Clitheroe, CC BY-SA 2.0), 198 (photo James T. M. Towill, CC BY-SA 2.0), 201 (photo Colin Park, CC BY-SA 2.0); © Robin Gillanders, reproduced by courtesy of the Estate of Ian Hamilton Finlay: p. 213; © Andy Goldsworthy: pp. 186, 187, 188; from Eugène Grasset, ed., *La Plante et ses applications ornementales* (Paris, 1901), vol. II, photo Zürcher Hochschule der Künste: p. 34; from James I, *Daemonologie* (London, 1603), photo Cornell University Library, Ithaca, NY: p. 85; Kaunas City Museum: p. 84; K. H. Renlund Museum, Kokkola: p. 75; from Andrew Laing, ed., *The Book of Romance* (New York, London and Bombay, 1903), photo New York Public Library: p. 49; Latvian National Museum of Art, Riga: p. 69; photo Colin McLean, reproduced with permission: p. 206; The McManus, Dundee's Art Gallery and Museum: pp. 120–21; The Metropolitan Museum of Art, New York: p. 30; from Alfred Moffat, ed., *The Minstrelsy of Scotland: 200 Scottish Songs, Adapted to Their Traditional Airs* (London, 1895): p. 106; photo Anna Moser, reproduced with permission: pp. 42–3; from Hilda Murray, *Flower Legends for Children* (London, New York and Bombay, 1901): p. 100; Musée d'Orsay, Paris: p. 76; Nasjonalmuseet, Oslo: p. 72 (photo Morten Thorkildsen, CC BY 4.0); National Folklore Collection, University

College Dublin (The Schools' Collection): p. 101 (vol. III, p. 161, CC BY-NC 4.0); National Library of Scotland, Edinburgh: p. 108 (CC BY 4.0); National Park Service (NPS): p. 11; Nordfjord Folkemuseum, Sandane: p. 32 (CC BY-SA 4.0); © Pitt Rivers Museum, University of Oxford: p. 88; Pixabay: p. 73 (NatashaG); private collection: pp. 93, 157; from Charles Rogers, ed., *Life and Songs of the Baroness Nairne* (Edinburgh, 1896): pp. 102, 105; from T. W. Rolleston, *Myths and Legends: The Celtic Race* (Boston, MA, 1910), photo Harold B. Lee Library, Brigham Young University, Provo, UT: p. 54; reproduced by permission of the Royal Irish Academy, Dublin, photo © RIA: p. 40 (MS 23 E 24, p. 116); from John Ruskin, *Modern Painters* (New York, 1885), vol. V, photo Harold B. Lee Library, Brigham Young University, Provo, UT: p. 143; from Viktor Rydberg, *Teutonic Mythology: Gods and Goddesses of the Northland* (London, 1906), vol. III: p. 63; Shutterstock.com: pp. 12 (*top*; Philip Bird LRPS CPAGB), 20–21 (Leonid Ikan), 56 (MNStudio), 65 (Veronika Hanzlikova), 74 (rook76), 89 (Paul Seftel), 97 (Stig Alenas), 109 (*bottom*; Jan Holm), 124 (Boris15), 149 (alanf); photos Oliver Southall: pp. 6, 9, 10, 13, 18, 46, 58, 83, 109 (*top*), 177, 180, 182, 184, 185; The State Hermitage Museum, St Petersburg: p. 35; The State Tretyakov Gallery, Moscow: p. 158; from Otto Wilhelm Thomé, *Flora von Deutschland, Österreich und der Schweiz* (Gera-Untermhaus, 1888), vol. III, photo ETH-Bibliothek Zürich: p. 15; Victoria and Albert Museum, London: p. 82; Walker Art Gallery, Liverpool: p. 138; Wellcome Collection, London: p. 38; Wikimedia Commons: pp. 8 (photo Frank Bothe, CC BY-SA 4.0), 12 (*middle* and *bottom*; photos Salvör Gissurardóttir, CC BY-SA 3.0), 47 (photo Kim Hansen, CC BY-SA 3.0), 59 (photo Christoph Radtke, CC BY 3.0), 80 (photo Ethan Doyle White, CC BY-SA 4.0), 160 and 165 (photos Vyacheslav Bukharov, CC BY-SA 4.0), 166 (Aleksiya Kosenko, CC BY-SA 4.0), 172 (public domain), 174 (Ivan, CC BY 3.0); from Thomas J. Wise, ed., *Letters from John Ruskin to Frederick J. Furnivall . . . and other correspondents* (London, 1897), photo courtesy Lilly Library, Indiana University, Bloomington, IN: p. 133; Yale Center for British Art, New Haven, CT: pp. 134, 135.

Index

꽃

Page numbers in *italics* refer to illustrations